Lifetime Lessons in Consulting

LIFETIME LESSONS IN CONSULTING

Stories, Anecdotes, and Lessons to Share

George Manning

Wisdom/Work
Published by Wisdom Work
TomVMorris.com

©2023 by George Manning
Designed by: Abigail Chiaramonte
Cover concept by: Kevin Warren

Library of Congress Cataloging-in-Publication Date February 2023
Names: Manning, George, author.
Title: Lifetime Lessons in Consulting: Stories, Anecdotes, and Lessons to Share | George Manning
Designation: First edition| Wilmington, North Carolina: Wisdom/Works [2023]

ISBN: 978-1-7377227-6-2
Subjects: 1. Business 2. Psychology

Printed in the United States of America

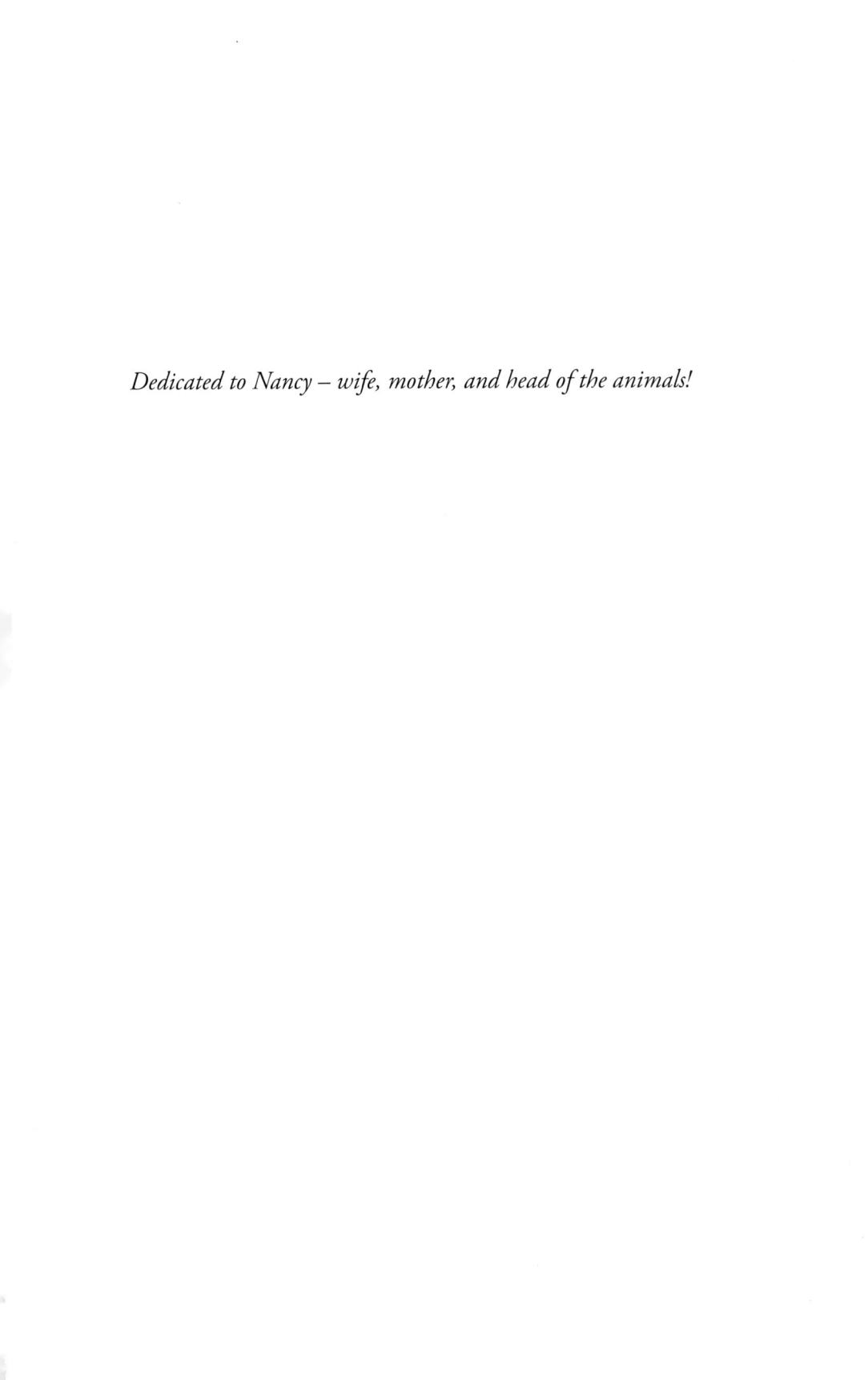

Dedicated to Nancy – wife, mother, and head of the animals!

Testimonials

This is an incredible resource. There is no area of organizational consulting that is not addressed. The most complex issues are synthesized into understandable principles and practices. The stories, references, and quotes are the icing on the cake. This book is a must-have for both new and experienced consultants.

– Rob Followell, Former CEO of
six hospitals and four healthcare systems

The author does a masterful job of describing the balance between theory and practice in organizational consulting. Reading this book is like receiving golf advice from Jack Nicklaus. Very few people have the depth and breadth of consulting experience that Professor Manning has. I highly recommend this text to students and practitioners who want to improve their consulting skills.

– Matthew Shank, President, Virginia Foundation
for Independent Colleges

There is an inner and outer game of consulting. The outer game is about strategy and models. The inner game is about self-knowledge, presence, and the ability to bring your best to any scenario. George Manning has been a role model for consultants for decades and his book is full of personal and professional insights. This book is a treasure for new consultants who want to accelerate their development and experienced consultants who want to "take it to the next level."

– *Gordon Barnhart, Management Consultant*

Lifetime Lessons in Consulting bridges the gap between learning and work and between behavior theory and business practice. It's a tremendous resource for graduate courses in organizational consulting and for anyone interested in consulting as a profession.

– *Gordon C. Duke, Secretary of Finance,*
Commonwealth of Kentucky

This is a work of rare, candid insight on self and occupation by a remarkable scholar and practitioner. *Lifetime Lessons in Consulting* is a delight to read. There are wonderfully crafted lessons here for all of us. This is a special gift to those involved in or thinking about becoming a mentor to organizations.

– *Lieutenant General Walter F. Ulmer, Jr.,*
U.S. Army (retired) and President of the
Center for Creative Leadership (retired)

As a former Professor of Leadership and Management, I love this book. It's not a textbook but rather a "learning" book that engages the reader in practical and useful ways. What fun!

– *Ken Blanchard, Author of* The One Minute Manager

The best teachers are those who show you where to look, but don't tell you what to see. Professor Manning was the best teacher I ever had! His passion for communicating real-life lessons from his experiences was terrific. I could not wait to sit in his classes & be allowed to visit the world of consulting that he created. Now I have the privilege to continue this journey through his writing of "Stories, Anecdotes, & Lessons to Share."

– *Ken Gunkel, Business Owner*

George Manning shares his journey as a professor and consultant. This book can be used as a course textbook (It's like a mini-education in itself) or as a practitioner's guide when addressing consulting issues. Anyone who enjoys honest self-reflection on a well-lived life will benefit from this engaging book. This book is a refreshing reminder of the value of decent and competent professionalism.

– *Joseph A. Petrick, Professor of Management and International Business, Wright State University*

Lifetime Lessons in Consulting is terrific. People love George Manning's original and authentic approach – so, too, with this book. Because I have read every book I could find on consulting, I know that both new and experienced consultants will benefit from reading this book.

– *Terri Bonar-Stewart, Management Consultant*

I've lived and worked in America, Europe, and Asia. In this business masterpiece, lessons are shared based on decades of teaching and consulting. It's a gift to oneself, and certainly to myself, to engage with Professor Manning's insights on leadership and influence.

– *Ling Xiao, Business Professor, University of Mannheim, Germany*

Lifetime Lessons in Consulting is an outstanding resource for consulting in today's business environment. It brings together all of the characteristics of good scholarship, teaching, and consulting.
– *Charles D. Leffler, Vice-Chancellor,*
North Carolina State University

One of the fundamental challenges of our time is developing ethical and wise people to lead our organizations. *Lifetime Lessons in Consulting* is a tremendous resource for professors and consultants to help address this need.
– *Larry Larson, Sorensen Family Dean -*
School of Engineering, Brown University

This book captures the imagination of anyone who aspires to be a consultant. As an experienced consultant, I was struck by what I didn't know and can now use to help my clients. George Manning epitomizes the term (A Life Well Lived) in service to others.
– *Nicholas J. Hun, Col U.S. Army (retired)*

This book is filled with wisdom and practical advice. It's a wonderful guide for anyone in the business of consulting or considering it. I've had the privilege of learning from George Manning, first as my university professor, and now as a friend and mentor in my own consulting firm. I'm excited about how helpful this book is to those in consulting!
– *Melody Rawlings, CEO, Meremel Group LLC*

Lifetime Lessons in Consulting is a continuation of George Manning's teaching philosophy and practice of consulting. This book is educational, but it's also inspiring. I've encouraged my colleagues and students to add this book to their professional libraries.
– *Mitchell Payne, National Forum for Black Public Administrators*

This is a "must-read" for those in the business of providing professional advice. The text outlines the characteristics and qualities of an effective consultant in an interactive and easy-to-read fashion. I have been in various physician leadership roles for nearly 50 years, and I regret not having this book at the beginning of my career. It's a thorough guidebook for successful consulting.
— *Donald Saelinger, Physician Executive*

This book covers key challenges facing organizational consultants with takeaways on problem-solving, creating a healthy organization, leading effective teams, developing leaders, and helping people through change. Readers can quickly access portions of the book when 'teachable moments' arise. The book is full of case studies and useful examples.
— *Kellie Guarino, Organizational Consultant*

As a Human Resource professional, I've relied on many resources to create a positive work culture. George Manning's books have been my top resource. Not only does this book provide an excellent roadmap for successful consulting, but it reminds organizational leaders what their role is really all about – people.
— *Tim Holbrook, Chief Human Resources Officer, Kentucky Legislative Research Commission*

If you are interested in becoming a consultant, or are already in practice, the author's expertise and demeanor will serve you well. I now have an exemplary resource to share with my former students when they ask, "Where can I learn about the consulting profession?" My reply will be, "I just happen to have the perfect book for you."
— *A. Charles Drubel, Professor Emeritus of Business, Muskingum University*

Leadership and organizational effectiveness have never been more important. George Manning is a trusted guide in the journey to serve our communities. The principles and practices shared in this book are helpful to both internal and external consultants in creating healthy and productive work environments.

– *William Harwood – Lieutenant Colonel,*
Maine State Police (retired)

Lifetime Lessons in Consulting is the most complete resource I have ever read about consulting. Professors, students, practitioners, and clients will enjoy and learn from the stories, lessons, and principles that are shared. The book is popular because it rings of truth based on more than fifty years of first-hand experience.

– *Fred Link, Management Consultant*

Effective consulting requires hard work, creativity, and a service mindset. The stories and lessons in this book are based on the life and work of a caring professional.

– *Earl Walz, Healthcare Executive*

Professors and students, as well as consultants and clients, will learn priceless lessons from this wonderful collection of experiences, principles, and practices. *Lifetime Lessons in Consulting* is a treasure for consulting effectiveness.

– *Susan Wehrspann, Author and Management Consultant*

I enjoyed this book tremendously. The application of the material is amazing. It's not only good for business, but it's extremely helpful in my family life as well. I've covered the book with notes, highlights, and sticky tabs. I plan on keeping it as is. It's one of those books you loan and make sure you ask for it back.

– *Paula Washburn, NKU Student*

Foreword

Tom Morris

    This book is an ideal guide for anyone who is early in a consulting career or is even considering such a form of work and life journey. It's also a book that will be enjoyed immensely by seasoned consultants and the executives who work with consultants, coaches, and advisors. Part memoir, part manual, it's written from the heart and mind of a most extraordinary man beloved by psychologists, philosophers, professors, corporate leaders, students, and huge numbers of people who work at every level in organizations throughout America and the broader world. It's as personal as it is professional, and that's the magic that makes it work.

    When I first read a draft of this wonderful book, I was astonished at how much one man can accomplish. As I read about George's vastly many clients, I sometimes felt that, while I have been living one fairly busy life, he somehow has managed to live five or six at once. How does anyone get so much done, over such a wide array of organizations and industries? I think the answer, as elusive as it might at first seem, is actually quite simple. He loves what he does, is energized by his clients, and he's always on the lookout for a new way to make a positive difference in the world. Plus, his career has been the epitome for "word of mouth" marketing. You do a great job, and people will hear about it and ask you to do more. As my wife has always warned me: "Be careful how well you do something. If it's really exceptional, everyone will be asking you to do more of it." George's career displays profoundly the inevitable results of being exceptional. He is a great guide and advisor for the rest of us in part because of the wide range of his experiences, and due to the example of wisdom and care he always brings to a challenge.

Of course, this paradigmatic and tremendously successful consultant has not done it alone. He's had partners and collaborators of all kinds along the way, from his wonderful wife Nancy, and on through scores of other very smart and talented people, individuals he credits lavishly in these stories. It's part of what then makes him a great partner for any reader. He knows how to share, how to give credit, the best ways to communicate, and he can always sense your next question or concern and give you just what you may need to tackle it. He doesn't think of himself as the great man he is, but would rather focus on helping you and me attain the greatness that still may await us.

It long puzzled me that the Roman emperor Marcus Aurelius began his famous "Notes to himself," better known in our time under the title, *Meditations*, with paragraph after paragraph thanking many mentors and influencers by name for this or that skill they showed him or lesson they taught him at various points in his life. I finally came to realize that he is helping us to see how we also need to operate, with a spirit of collaboration, of partnership with others, and a deep sense of gratitude toward the many people who aid us along the way. This is exactly the mindset that will help us approach the next opportunity of partnership with a delighted and positive expectation for lessons to be learned, wisdom to be imparted, and good to be done. It's also a great spirit to bring to this book in order to extract all its lessons, its real wisdom, and the good it can help make possible in your own life.

It's only in recent years that I've come to recognize how much great world literature is about the power of partnership. It's one of the main themes of the *Iliad*, and enlivens such otherwise very different books as *The Three Musketeers* and Bram Stoker's *Dracula*. A difficulty that one lone individual might find to be utterly impossible to manage can often be handled quite successfully by several people in collaboration, when they bring their diverse perspectives and strengths to the challenge. George's recollections in this book often reflect that truth. He has had great collaborators, and he clearly has been a great partner for many. He will become yours through these pages and stories.

The author of this delightful book is also one of the most supportive and encouraging people I've ever met. That spirit also comes through in everything he does. You will find yourself supported and encouraged by his words and insights throughout the book. George Manning is, to use a famous phrase, "a man for others," and one of the most wonderful joys and ironies of life is that this has provided him with an incredible adventure of his own.

Table of Contents

Introduction   1

#1 The early years – Philosophy and Psychology as foundational disciplines   5

#2 The second most important year of my life, 1963-64 – University of Vienna, Oscar Robertson, Viktor Frankl, and Israeli Kibbutzim   6

#3 False start in Arkansas and UC (University of Cincinnati) salvation   12

#4 Lucien Cohen, I/O (Industrial/Organizational) Psychology, and Eureka on I-75!   14

#5 First challenge to teach – from swimming pool lifeguard to University of Cincinnati/University of Dayton instructor (with Jenny Bean out of sight)   17

#6 Stress interview – General Motors and Ralph Nader (failure and lessons learned)   19

#7 Graduation and first adult job – Milacron, Kroger, and Ford (I go with Ford under false pretenses)   21

#8 The most important year of my life, 1967 – career, marriage, new baby, first home, University of Cincinnati doctoral program   22

#9 Mistakes of commission – the Ford years   25

#10 The third most important year of my life, 1970 – Executive General, NKU (Northern Kentucky University), and life as I have known it for 52 years   28

#11 Five early decisions that proved to be good   33

#12 The absolute need to live and work by five core principles for consulting success   39

#13 The importance of questions   41

#14 How teaching helps consulting and vice-versa   43

#15 Working unfettered – consulting success and the ghost in the machine   49

#16 The brain, the terrain, and creating your future– Ben Carson's story   51

#17 Consulting partnerships where one and one is more than two   55

#18 The asexual consultant   67

#19 My list of mosts   69

#20 Large scale consulting   77

#21 Number one consulting skill – time management	87
#22 The Stabilus story – cross cultural communication and business success, including the SPOT (Superior Products on Time) manifesto	90
#23 Train the trainer initiatives	92
#24 Going Hollywood – Sara Lee, Dolly Parton, and the stress of change (summer in the dark room)	98
#25 Most stressful groups	100
#26 What I didn't know that I wish I did know	105
#27 Be prepared – the motto of a good scout (the importance of knowing a day in the life of the client)	108
#28 The consultant image – the eye of the beholder	111
#29 Reality and humble pie	114
#30 Be a continuous learner (every teacher needs a teacher)	115
#31 Evaluation criteria for consulting services	120
#32 Joe Ward, Jimmy Stewart, and the Toyota news story – the power of the pen	122
#33 The 4th most important year of my life, 2000 – the stern and craggy shores of Maine	124

#34 Using outdoor initiatives as a personal growth/OD (Organizational Development) tool – limits, liabilities, and testimonials … 126

#35 Consulting for trade – barbecue ribs, hotel hospitality, and dental care … 130

#36 Attention and effort – work to learn/work to remember … 133

#37 SERDI (Southeast Regional Directors Institute) lifelong learning – 911, Government Accounting 101, and Virginia's Black Box … 135

#38 Dodging Stones – Courts, Corrections, and CitiCorp … 136

#39 Stretched in Nashville – the night it couldn't be done … 138

#40 Be a learner – the importance of books … 140

#41 Every consultant's dilemma – how much to charge … 143

#42 Records count – keep them! … 148

#43 Consultant-client compact … 149

#44 The fit consultant … 153

#45 The need for mindfulness … 159

#46 Client personalities … 161

#47 No turtle ever got on a fencepost by itself – staff support   165

#48 Diversity as a strength   167

#49 The balance of theory and practice   169

#50 Managing human capital   172

#51 Technology challenges   174

#52 The theory and practice of leadership – balance is best   176

#53 Problem solving and human relations – two magic keys (the skeleton key/the master key)   178

#54 Murphy's Law   181

#55 Maine projects and activities   184

#56 A nod to Freud   187

#57 My best two leaders   189

#58 How writing helps consulting and vice-versa   190

#59 The Red River Leadership Institute – the strength of a region (building community without losing culture)   196

#60 Golf course pearls – make your last work your best work   198

#61 Don't take yourself too seriously   199

#62 Coping with change – the path of a book   200

#63 Career advice – straight shots, zig zags, and loop arounds   202

#64 Handling stressful situations   204

#65 Unexpected loss and the Phoenix Phenomenon – from overhead projector to flash drive   205

Conclusion   207

Appendix A – Books   209

Appendix B – Syllabus   216

Appendix C – Lessons Learned   229

Appendix D – Timeline and Code (Biography, Principles, Relationships, Cases)   242

Index   246

About the Author   256

Introduction

The safecracker Willie Sutton said, "We live our lives three ways – how we remember them, what we tell others, and what really happened." The stories in this book are true, and each has a lesson to share. This book has three audiences: my family who may be wondering what I've been doing all these years; friends and colleagues who are participants in these stories; and anyone who may be curious – what does a consultant do?

A consultant is defined as anyone who provides expert advice professionally (from Latin: consultare "to deliberate"). It is an old line of work with examples of Merlin who advised King Arthur, Aristotle who counseled Alexander the Great, and Chanakya who taught Chandragupta. It can be argued that the best consulting is provided by parents. Abraham Lincoln traced his leadership principles to the advice of his two Mothers, Nancy Hanks and Sarah Bush Johnston.

Most consulting for pay is done for organizations and individuals in the private, public, and non-profit sectors of society. The market size of the U.S. management consulting industry, measured by revenue, is 329.1 bn in 2022. This has grown 5.1 % per year on average between 2017 and 2022, increasing faster than the U.S. economy overall. The leading revenue generators for the industry in the United States are in management, scientific, and technical consulting services. In general, consultants provide information, diagnose problems, recommend actions, and help implement solutions.

There are many kinds of consultants who help others achieve their goals. Business, finance, engineering, marketing, IT, and human resource consultants abound. Consultants are active in every art and science, and every industry, profession, and trade. Examples include career consultants, life coaches, and political advisors. Some work in large consulting firms, others work in specialty groups, and some work independently. Each structure can be effective for the client, and each can be satisfying for the consultant. Three giants in management consulting were Peter Drucker, Douglas McGregor, and James O. McKinsey. All three were good consultants, but each preferred a different approach to serving his clients – *individual* Peter Drucker, *group practice* Douglas McGregor, and *large firm* McKinsey & Company.

Consulting is a robust industry. As of 2022, there are 1,121,512 management consulting businesses in the U.S., employing 2,160,836 people. There are over 499,861 consultants currently employed (58.4 percent men, 41.6 percent women). The average age of an employed consultant is 43 years old. There are large consulting companies with thousands of employees like McKinsey & Company, Boston Consulting Group, Bain & Company, Deloitte, PricewaterhouseCoopers, KPMG, Ernst & Young, and there are boutique firms specializing in focused services and markets that have hundreds of employees. The average U.S. management consulting firm is a small business with relatively few employees.

This book tells the experience of just one consultant – me. The stories span fifty-two years as a professor with an active consulting practice speaking, teaching, advising, and writing about the human side of work. As a management and organization consultant, my focus has been on work morale and productivity, with areas of interest in leadership, ethics, communication, motivation, stress, and change. A third of my work has been public speaking, a third has been organization development, and a third has been corporate training in these areas. Fifty percent of my clients have been private companies, thirty percent have been government organizations, and twenty percent have been professions, trades, and associations. When asked why did you write a 'first person' book, most people say, it's mostly for me – either I enjoyed remembering things, or I enjoyed writing it all down. I enjoyed both.

The origin of this book is a graduate course I teach in organizational consulting using a good text, *The Contemporary Consultant* by Larry Greiner, and a good reader, *The Consultant's Calling* by Geoffrey Bellman. My friend and colleague Bill Attenweiler helped me create a great syllabus featuring panels with experts in strategy and organization, marketing, operations, computer and information systems, and human resource consulting, as well as panels of users of consulting services (buyers and gatekeepers). During the last half-hour of each three-hour class, random numbers are called 1 - 65, allowing various stories and anecdotes to be told by the instructor, including what happened and lessons learned. The spontaneity is stimulating, topics are current, and discussion is often continued over a beverage or two.

A book written in the first person walks a fine line between being an ego trip and being a helpful personal account for others to read and use. In 1965, I read *Lives in Progress* by Robert White. I can still remember the central characters, their stories, and the lessons they learned. All of the stories in this book are based on my personal experiences, but the lessons I learned can be useful to any consultant anywhere and anytime. Like an old Cracker Jack box with a surprise inside, there is always a lesson to learn.

How to read this book? Skip around and read what sounds interesting or useful. It is not meant to be read in sequence, cover to cover. Write in the margins; make the book yours. Use two highlighters – one for others, one for you. The entire compilation is a smörgåsbord of information coded B-biographic, P-principles, C-cases, and R-relationships. Like potato chips, hopefully you won't be able to stop with just one.

The stories in this book are presented in the general order of occurrence. An average of 80 consulting days per year for over 50 years equals more than 4,000 interventions, no two of which are the same. Another description for the book could be vignettes in the life of a consultant, or portrait of a consultant's life. To say consulting is both demanding and fulfilling is an understatement. The tagline of this book could be *Never a dull moment, Oh My!* Nothing would be more accurate, as these stories, anecdotes, and lessons to share will reveal. Also, nothing could be more satisfying. Here we go!

#1

The Early Years – Philosophy and Psychology as Foundational Disciplines

Lesson 1. Having fundamental knowledge about a subject is important to being a successful consultant. Majoring in philosophy (the study of what is real, true, and valuable) and psychology (the study of why people do what they do) was a tremendous help for me. These disciplines provide foundational theories and themes that underpin the human side of work. It's been important to know the philosophers in Bertrand Russell's *History of Western Philosophy*, the theories of behaviorism, psychoanalysis, and humanistic psychology, and the works of thought leaders in management and organizational behavior.

Lesson 2. It's important to stay current in one's field. Issues, studies, findings, and applications evolve in every field, and the effective consultant will remain fully knowledgeable and competent. Like a physical structure that needs a solid foundation and excellent construction, the successful consultant must have a strong philosophy of practice and highly effective methods of application to be current.

#2

The Second Most Important Year of My Life, 1963-64 – University of Vienna, Oscar Robertson, Viktor Frankl, and Israeli Kibbutzim

The second most important year of my life started in New York City with a welcome speech by the Dean of the Institute of European Studies. I had never seen or heard such a charismatic figure as Ed Mowatt, as he described the year ahead, the academic year of 1963-1964. From his talk, I knew it would be great, hard, and exciting. I learned how great it was when I boarded the Queen Elizabeth Ocean liner the next morning, and I discovered how hard it would be when I went below to my assigned cabin and met six classmates (there were 40 students in the Vienna program). I barely understood a word they said even in English, and when they spoke in German, I was mortified. These were students from prestigious schools, and I felt like a duck in a fox camp. I rushed to the main deck as fast as I could to get off the ship, but it had left the dock and we were passing the Statue of Liberty. All I could think of was failure ahead. When I returned to my cabin, I met two fellows, Erhard Linnes and Gordon Barron, who became my salvation.

The Vienna year began with 4 days of classes on the ship and 10 days of study in England, France, Belgium, Holland, Luxembourg, and Germany. The subjects were history, art, architecture, politics, language, and social customs. When we arrived in Vienna, we were required to pass a day of exams, or be sent home. I wouldn't have passed these exams if it were not for the intense tutoring of Erhard, who was raised in Germany till age 10, when he moved to America, and Gordon, who had lived and traveled in Europe almost every summer of his life. It was a leap from Middletown, Ohio to college in Chicago, and it was like space travel to study for a year in a foreign country. This proved to be a time of enormous change for me. When I returned to New York a year later on the Queen Mary, my mother was happy to see me, while my father couldn't help thinking I was ruined. My mind wasn't the same, we saw things differently, and it was difficult to talk. I'll be forever grateful to my parents who allowed me this great adventure.

As a student, I learned many lessons in the second most important year of my life, but three major ones were: 1. The value of experiencing another culture; 2. The importance of keeping an open mind; and 3. People make life worth living. I learned to visit foreign places, be personally humble, and make good friends. The following are 13 snapshots in an album of experiences, a baker's dozen. Each of these experiences enriched me and prepared me for my future career:

1. I changed my major in college to philosophy which resulted in new beliefs. Although I couldn't get Ed Mowatt to change my C grade in Greek Moral Philosophy, I was thoroughly inspired to think deeply and live accordingly. Studying philosophy led to Athens, Jerusalem, and Rome.

2. I added a second major in psychology primarily due to Viktor Frankl, who became a lifelong teacher. His book *Man's Search for Meaning* and his lectures on Logotherapy

resonated with me. Frankl thought everyone needs a purpose in life, something important to do. He thought everything we do goes down in history and is irretrievable. His prescription was to live a meaningful life that was self-transcendent and helpful to others.

3. Vienna changed my pace in the course of a year. I was goal-driven, achievement-oriented, and always on task when I arrived. Daily life in Austria is much slower and interactions are relaxed. The term for this is *gemutlichkeit* meaning to be agreeably pleasant, at ease, and enjoy the moment. By the time I left, I could smell roses in the Stadtpark and walk with a friend without feeling guilty.

4. Four fellows lived with Frau Zimmerman, who treated us like a grandmother. She cared about us, and we cared about her. Omi was old enough to have danced the Walz in the court of Emperor Franz Joseph l. We took her to American gangster movies and westerns with German sub-titles. Al Capone and John Wayne were her favorites. I will always remember her laughter and kindness. I made her American pancakes one day, which she loved.

5. When John F. Kennedy was shot on November 22, the world was stunned and filled with grief. The sadness I saw in the eyes of the Austrian people was as if a beloved son of their own had been killed. Along with countless Viennese, I went to St. Stephen's Cathedral to mourn his passing and honor his life.

6. For exercise, I rode my bike to the University of Vienna gymnasium, where I discovered a third string basketball

player from a small college in the U.S. could play the sport better than Austrian players at that time, just like most Austrian soccer players could be stars in America. I was like Oscar Robertson in Vienna, and I learned everyone should be a hero sometime. Playing basketball also allowed me to eat a lot of Viennese pastry, because I could run it off quickly.

7. Hitchhiking, train trips, river cruises, and youth hostels were learning excursions, often with a true friend, Bobbi. Trips to Salzburg, Innsbruck, Munich, Heidelberg, Amsterdam, Dusseldorf, Bonn, Hamburg, and Nuremberg were glorious adventures, although frostbite was a factor hitchhiking in the winter.

8. Climbing Hafalakar in Innsbruck, hiking Zugspitze in Bavaria, and Christmas skiing in Kaprun, Austria were exhilarating experiences, except when my friend Erhard broke his leg near the top of the mountain over Kaprun. We were the last skiers to leave the top and it was getting dark quickly. I stayed with Erhard while Bill Gebbie raced down the mountain to get help from the village rescue team. The moonlight view from the cable car was stunning, although Erhard doesn't remember it or the Saint Bernard rescue dog either.

9. A trip to Prague, Czechoslovakia in the winter was sobering. Under Communist rule at the time, Prague was drab, and the people were depressed in contrast to colorful and vibrant Vienna, a sister city of the same historical era. Once picturesque and charming, Prague looked and felt oppressive in 1964. A chance friendship developed with a Prague

physician and his family that resulted in their later move to America. I was careful not to do anything controversial in Prague, for fear of arrest.

10. For winter break, I left Vienna for a long trip through Hungary and Yugoslavia to Greece, then to Turkey and Israel, then back to Greece and Vienna. The Grand Bazaar in Istanbul and a Turkish freighter to Haifa kept me on my toes as a traveler alone in foreign places. At a port call in Izmir, Turkey, there was a U.S. Army station, and I had a cheeseburger and fries, my first in six months. Imagine my joy! When I left Vienna, the father of my Persian friend Shari gave me a sheepskin vest. Then, when I was in a small store in Israel, three young fellows took it from me. There are nice people and jerks in every country.

11. My goal for winter break was to work on a Kibbutz in Israel. I arrived at Kfar Menachem unannounced, and they welcomed me graciously. It was a significant experience. I picked grapefruits and oranges in the fields and learned the history and sociology of Kibbutzim in the evening. Kibbutzim is collective communal living and democratic governance as a way of life. Religion varies in importance in different Kibbutzim. Most dramatic to me was that my friend Israel viewed the Kibbutz as his primary family, even more than his biological parents. I have never seen or tasted such big and sweet grapefruits and oranges in my life!

12. Italy was highly educational, although I missed the Pope in Rome because a young lady was willing to take a Vespa trip. Seeing Rome as well as visiting Venice, Florence, Pisa, Assisi, Naples, the French Riviera, and Monaco made indelible

Spring memories. About studies – I always studied with a book in one hand and a notepad in the other, no matter where I was. I was determined to do well in school so that all of my courses at the University of Vienna would transfer as credits toward graduation.

13. There is nothing like an opera, if one has never seen an opera, especially in Vienna. The city ranks at the top of music and theater culture in the world. The Vienna Symphony and The Vienna Boys' Choir are examples, and the Vienna State Opera is the crown jewel. Studienplatz standing room tickets cost very little and if one stood in line, the reward was seeing such operas as La Traviata, Carmen, La Boheme, The Magic Flute, and The Barber of Seville. This was a whole new experience for a Midwest American teenager, and I enjoyed it immensely.

Each of these experiences gave me a broader sensibility toward life and a deeper sensitivity to the wide variety of people to be found in it.

#3

False Start in Arkansas and UC (University of Cincinnati) Salvation

As a college senior in 1965, I had to decide what would be next: 1. The Peace Corps in Cameroon Africa sounded perfect until I learned it was a three-year assignment. I had just returned from a year in Austria, and I didn't want to be away for three more years. 2. Joining Kellogg or Upjohn Pharmaceutical as a management trainee sounded good, in terms of a stable career path, or good beginning, but not personally meaningful at the time. 3. Graduate school in Psychology at the University of Arkansas seemed just right. I chose graduate school and moved to Fayetteville, Arkansas, rented an apartment, signed up for classes, and went to a Lovin' Spoonful rock concert.

During the second week of class, I asked the Department Chair, where are the people? Where are the psychology subjects? Discussions were focused on research methods, experimental design, statistical tools, data collection, reinforcement schedules, and animal care; and human behavior hadn't been mentioned. That's when I learned I was in an Experimental Psychology program and was a fish in the wrong pond. The 'know when to hold them, know when to fold them' lyrics best described my situation.

I realized I had made a mistake and was in the wrong place due to some false assumptions. Adding to this was daily news about the Viet Nam War. I was lucky to be an American and I felt a sense of duty to serve my country. The combination of being in the wrong place and wanting to do the right thing impelled me to hitchhike home to Ohio and join the military. I enjoyed the trip with a trucker, especially because the Ozark Mountains are beautiful in a primordial way.

I went to the Federal Building in Cincinnati intending to join the Navy, but my eyesight was so poor, and my feet were so flat that I was rejected by the Navy, Marines, Army, and Air Force. I think they were worried that I would lose my glasses, shoot my friends, and be unable to march. In short, I would be a hazard, not a help. When I walked out of the Federal Building with a 1-Y classification, I was dejected and goalless. Then, Grandma Moses' advice kicked in: Life is what you make it . . . always was, always will be. I knew I should find a graduate program in psychology that focused on people as quickly as possible. I did this at the University of Cincinnati beginning the next quarter of the academic year.

I learned two lessons from the false start in Arkansas and the UC salvation: 1. Get the facts before making a decision. 2. Be true to yourself and you can't be false to others. When you are doing the wrong thing, stop; when you are in the wrong place, leave. Even with poor eyesight and flat feet, you can still see where the fit isn't right and walk away. These lessons are critical for effective consulting.

#4

Lucien Cohen, I/O (Industrial/Organizational) Psychology, and Eureka on I-75!

Lucien Cohen taught Industrial-Organizational Psychology at the University of Cincinnati. Every big city in America at that time had a Lucien Cohen, a master at applying psychology in the work environment. I took his courses in 1966 and he asked me to work in his I/O practice. Until then, I knew nothing about the world of work. I knew camp counseling, lifeguarding, and bartending as an employee, but I had no idea about the business world. I barely knew the difference between an engineer and an accountant. As for I/O psychology, I didn't know tests and measurements, work design and morale, psychological profiles and counseling, attitude surveys, pay and reward systems, or training and development. It was all new to me . . . and enjoyable to learn.

Watching Lucien work was like watching a master bricklayer or composer. He knew the science of his profession and he was an artist as he worked with his industrial and individual clients – always with a successful outcome. It was eye-opening and highly interesting to see consulting at its best as he helped people be productive and fulfilled in their work lives. Lucien was a mentor to me for over 20 years. It's important to have such a person in your life, to give guidance and encouragement.

When you are young or new in a field, seek an experienced mentor. This will turbo-charge your development. Even if you are shy or worried about imposing, and even if your mentor is busy or introverted, don't wait to be picked. The spark of learning will result in a satisfying and productive relationship for both you and your mentor.

One day that year, I had a life-defining sequence of thoughts while I was driving past the General Electric Plant on I-75. Both Karl Marx and Abraham Lincoln believed that how a society does its work determines most other things about the society, including community life, family life, and personal life. I found their thoughts about the importance of work to be insightful. People all over the world spend an enormous amount of time at work. Regarding my own life, I knew experimental and clinical psychology were not good fits for me. But I thought if I could help people have positive and healthy work lives including high morale and high performance, that would be good. Oliver Wendell Holmes, Jr. said a mind stretched by a new idea never returns to its original dimension. Karl Marx and Abraham Lincoln stretched my mind in 1966.

As a philosophy major, I cared about the human condition and understood the importance of man's search for meaning as emphasized by Viktor Frankl. As a psychology major, I wanted to help make work meaningful for people, much like Lucien Cohen did in his I/O practice. I thought helping people have high morale and high performance in their work lives would help them in their personal, family, and community lives as well. This would be a life worth living.

My sequence of thoughts on I-75 resulted in deciding on a niche and calling. It gave me clarity of purpose that has guided me for over 56 years. It gave me peace of mind to think I was doing the right thing, for the right reason, in the right way, at the right time. It was a Eureka moment! **The lesson I learned was that each person's niche is unique, ranging from art to science, to serving the needs of others. Finding one's niche or calling is fundamental to a satisfying and productive life for every person, and I wanted to help.**

#5

First Challenge to Teach – from Swimming Pool Lifeguard to University of Cincinnati/University of Dayton Instructor (With Jenny Bean Out of Sight)

In the summer of 1966, I was working as a lifeguard in the day and a bartender in the evening when Bill Stewart of the University of Cincinnati asked me to teach a course on Human Relations for the Dayton Foreman's Club. I had just gained clarity of purpose in I/O Psychology and wanted to do such an assignment. I was half the age of most class participants, but excellent coursewares, the desire to teach, and the patience of the class made for a grand success. I was asked to teach a similar course at Hobart Manufacturing in Troy, Ohio; then two courses in Supervision at Piqua and Hamilton, Ohio.

Preparing to teach these subjects and conducting classes up and down the Miami Valley for four years were tremendous growth experiences, all traced to Bill Stewart's trust and encouragement. Dr. Stewart also became a life-long mentor with colorful stories that were usually told with spaghetti sauce and cigar ashes on his shirt, once-a-week lunches listening to my experiences and anxieties as a young father and labor representative, and full backing in my pursuit of a Doctoral degree.

Dr. Stewart wasn't much of a researcher, and I never knew for sure if what he said was true – he once told me he had discovered the number one factor that correlated with success as a leader was being an Eagle Scout. It made some sense to me because the self-discipline to earn the merit badges and supportive parents who would drive you to merit badge meetings were potent forces for success. The doors Bill Stewart opened and the encouragement he gave me were gifts for life. When I completed my degree, Dr. Stewart became the most serious I ever saw him, when he said: "You've been a taker till now and people have helped you succeed. Now, you must focus on others and 'pass it on.' " He also said, "If you are all wrapped up in yourself, you're overdressed."

A personal experience happened that summer when Jenny B., a young lady attending Ohio University, made it clear that I wasn't her favorite. **James Brown was singing *I Feel Good*, but I learned a broken heart can hurt as much as a broken leg. I also learned hearts heal quickly and aches are temporary when people are young, so don't do anything foolish. Experiences like this have helped me understand the lives of young people for 52-plus years.**

#6

Stress Interview – General Motors and Ralph Nader (Failure and Lessons Learned)

I discovered Industrial/Organizational Psychology (I/O) in 1966 and loved everything about it. I learned to do the work by watching and being taught by a master of the practice, Lucien Cohen. Applying psychology to the world of work was an ideal fit for my undergraduate majors in philosophy and psychology. I took graduate courses in leadership with William Stewart and grew immensely from teaching human relations and leadership courses for the University of Cincinnati. In the Fall of 1966, General Motors had an opening in labor relations at its Norwood assembly plant. The University of Cincinnati career services and the Norwood Labor Relations Department recommended me for the position, and I was sent to Detroit for a final interview.

I failed miserably in Detroit where I was given a stress interview in a dark room on a hot and raised spot-lit stage. Business, automobile, and human resource questions were asked, and I didn't know the answers, including questions about the safety issue with General Motors' Corvair automobile. I didn't know who Ralph Nader was and I didn't know the name of his book on automobile safety, *Unsafe at Any Speed.* I experienced the signs and effects of stress that I would study and write about 10 years later. I was clearly inadequate to fill the position and was dismissed summarily. I returned to Cincinnati with a note that said – *prepare properly.* It was embarrassing and I was thoroughly ashamed. I had been a Boy Scout, but I violated the #1 rule of a good scout – In any situation, be prepared!

It's said that life is 10% what happens to you and 90 % how you handle it. **I learned to prepare properly for all future business meetings, including a job interview. I learned the importance of being able to say yes to three questions: Can you do the job at the level of deliverable required? Do you want to do the job? Is this position a good psycho-social fit for you?** My answers were 'no' to all three questions at General Motors in 1966.

#7

Graduation and First Adult job – Milacron, Kroger, and Ford (I Go With Ford Under False Pretenses)

I completed a master's degree in December 1966 and looked forward to working in human resources. My goal was to apply what I had learned in I/O Psychology from Lucien Cohen and leadership from Bill Stewart. I was offered a position with Cincinnati Milacron, The Kroger Company, and The Ford Motor Company. The companies were equally appealing, but I chose Ford because the opportunity for growth seemed enormous. **Regarding graduation: Students often ask – walk or don't walk? I always say walk. Graduation isn't just for graduates; it's also for those who care about them and want to celebrate their success.**

Lesson for life: The three most important questions facing a young person are 1. Who are you? 2. What do you want to do? 3. Who do you want to be with? Problems come when one addresses these questions out of order. I was thankful I answered questions 1 and 2 by December 1966 before meeting my wife Nancy in January 1967 and starting a family.

#8

The Most Important Year of My Life, 1967 – Career, Marriage, New Baby, First Home, University of Cincinnati Doctoral Program

The single most important year of my life was 1967. December, 1966 started things rolling because I completed a master's degree from the University of Cincinnati and was hired as a labor representative at Ford Motor Company. I moved to a great new apartment in Clifton and bought a 1966 candy apple red Thunderbird convertible. Then, on January 4, 1967, I met my wife Nancy and our two sons, Page and Larry. Everything changed! We were married two months later in March and moved to a rented home across the road from the Spring Grove Cemetery, which, for some reason, we loved. Our daughter Heather was born in December of that year at Christ Hospital. Seeing Heather for the first time is the most vivid memory of my life. Heather* completed our family, as Leonhard Dowty writes:

> Our house is filled with many joys:
> A playful pup, a pair of boys,
> A fireside warm and cozy,
> An easy chair soft and dozy,

Lots of gadgets automatic,
That wash and whisk and whip and whirl –
And one enchanting little girl.

By the end of 1967, I started a doctoral program at the University of Cincinnati. I saw the need for a terminal degree as security for my family. In our first year of marriage, a thought came to me that guided my life – I make the living because Nancy makes the living worthwhile. A similar thought came to me 23 years later when Nancy had a stroke. I found an antique picture that said, "What's a home without a mother?" As for Nancy, the two sayings that helped her with me were, "Be careful what you pray for, you might get it," and, "He's a work in progress."

1967 began 50-plus years together as a working Dad, homemaking Mom, and three great kids. This was the most important year of my life because it focused on family activities with traditional values. Pets too many to name included dogs Teddy and Toby, cats Pussycat and Pooka, horses Meadow Spring and Honeybee, birds Jay-bee and Henry, and a goat named Nanny. Typical outings were picnics, creek bottoms, beaches, drive-in movies, antique stores, dinners together, and every holiday and birthday celebration. Our lives were full and happy as a family beginning this wonderful year.

Many people have an image of business consultants as always on the move, living in hotels and airports, nearly rootless except in ideas and clients. But good soil and firm roots in a home life worth having are important for a sane and healthy consultant. Homes and families may look very different, but it's vital to have your own metaphorical version of a hearth, with family or close friends in nurturing, supportive relationships.

Every family has a list. Our grand adventures included: 1. Ohio's oldest Inn, the Golden Lamb, every Thanksgiving and Easter and six months in 1977; 2. Bears in the Smokey Mountains; 3. Vacation at Sodus Point, New York on Lake Ontario; 4. Multiple state parks in Ohio, Kentucky, Tennessee, and Indiana; 5. 40 years of horses (20 years of shows); 6. We loved walking and snow-sledding in Spring Grove Cemetery; 7. The great Frog-Jumping Contest that Page and Larry won with contestants from the cemetery pond. These were eventful times that we will always remember.

Parenting is demanding and so is working – there is only so much room in a coffee cup. Our children have been healthy, happy, loving, and respectful all their lives, thank goodness. Nancy was a full-time homemaker, and our children have not been sick or difficult. This has allowed me the time required to work hard, go to school, and advance professionally.

In 1967, I learned the three keys to happiness: having someone to love, having something important to do, and counting my blessings. Another lesson I learned in 1967 was how challenging it would be to earn a living and raise a family. I remember thinking as I was mowing the lawn one Saturday: Managing a career isn't too bad. Deadlines and all of the meetings are fine. I can handle being a father to two boys and a new baby girl. Being a husband and spending time with Nancy is great. The work of keeping up a home is OK too. It's doing all of these things at the same time that's killing me. I hope I can keep it up.

* How do I describe our daughter today? She lights up a room. She's a natural-born mother. She lives life like someone left the gate open. She's precious!

#9

Mistakes of Commission – The Ford Years

In 1966, I was hired by Ford Motor Company under false pretenses; by 1967, I was almost fired. In 1969, at a celebration dinner, John Condon told me the company hired me by mistake. Ford salaried personnel director Harry Kleintop thought I was one of 16 children and could succeed in labor relations. When I proceeded to make mistake after mistake, it was discovered that my dad was one of 16 children, but I was an only child.

It came to a head when I mistakenly sent the midnight shift assembly department home, and zero versus 1,300 transmissions were made that night. It was the last straw. Industrial Relations wanted to fire me, but Operations Management said no – you hired him, make it work. Jim Brooks, a 350 pound Labor Relations legend, was willing to train me, and took me on as a project. As Yogi Berra said, you can observe a lot by watching, and I improved with Jim's example and encouragement. He was wise and patient and saved my young career. Jim was the man who drove me to the Central Trust Bank to open my first checking account and deposit my first Ford check. I experienced again the importance of mentors in the world of work and the broader world of life.

Mistake 1: Frank Pandorf (safety glasses) – I received a call from a production department where an angry dispute was in progress. In my rush, I forgot to wear safety glasses. Labor Relations was enforcing safety glasses and the area production superintendent took obvious pleasure in dressing me down. He later apologized and took the time to help me understand the importance of my mistake.

Mistake 2: Jessie Bowling (union representation) – While conducting a disciplinary action with an employee, the supervisor and union steward were arguing, so I dismissed them both and completed the hearing alone with the employee. This was a big mistake and the incident escalated to Solidarity House, the UAW's headquarters in Detroit.

Mistake 3: Dying in the file cabinet (Lee Iacocca's employment goal and Sam Sheppard's cellmate) – The lack of stimulation in a personnel department assignment almost killed me until Lee Iacocca launched a nationwide initiative to hire the hard-core unemployed and I was charged to do this for our location. I loved the challenge and saw it as a meaningful initiative. When the cellmate of convicted killer Sam Sheppard applied for work, I hired him immediately. When upper management learned of this, they said I was over-zealous.

Mistake 4: Hi-Tavern (the night daddy ate a bad sandwich) – Jim Brooks, my Labor Relations mentor, was a big man and could drink a lot. I was a young fellow who didn't drink but wanted to be accepted. When Jim drank a shot, I did too. When he drank a second and third, I did too. I don't remember the fourth shot, but I do remember Nancy and the kids coming to get me and take me home. I remember her telling the boys I ate a bad sandwich.

As a corrective action for these and a few other mistakes of commission, I was assigned to the company shoe store for seasoning and study. I knew I was at a low point and was faced with the three choices in life: give up, give in, or give it all you've got. I didn't know who said it at the time, but I followed the advice of Teddy Roosevelt and chose number three. This was reinforced by a quote I read attributed to Henry Ford: Failure is simply the opportunity to begin again with more intelligence. I redeemed myself by cleaning the store and launching a successful safety shoe sales campaign. Instead of thinking there is no market for safety shoes because no one wears them, I thought the market is enormous because no one wears safety shoes. **Lesson learned: second chances are good if you take responsibility, have a positive attitude, learn from mistakes, and work hard.**

I loved my years at Ford. They grew me like a weed. I had successes, such as coordinating the Skilled Trades Apprenticeship Program, coordinating the Management Education Program, and Labor Relations shift responsibility. Plus, I learned a ton from the experiences I had and the mistakes I made. First hand experiences prepared me well for what I would go on one day to do. We all need preparation. It may take different forms. But it's hard to leap into consulting without any special experience, or range of experience to give you a dollop of wisdom and some empathy for the plight of others.

#10

The Third Most Important Year of My Life, 1970 – Executive General, NKU (Northern Kentucky University), and Life as I Have Known it for 52 Years

In 1968, the Ford plant in Sharonville began a reduction in force. By early 1969, I was the youngest in seniority in Labor Relations and was given two choices – transfer to Detroit or take a job layoff. The pluses of transfer were promotion and income; the minus was not finishing a doctoral degree, including the long-term security I thought it would bring. The plus of layoff was completing the degree; the minus was immediate economic uncertainty. I chose door two, but the only employers who would hire me were consulting firms. At that time, I didn't know what consulting was, but it sounded shady to me. When two firms asked me to join them, my suspicion was confirmed. People would hire me to provide services about which I knew little. I had a wife and three children, so I said yes to the consulting firm Executive General, hoping to learn quickly.

Consulting at Executive General was a good fit. The three owners, Compton Allen, Roger Grimshaw, and Bill Holloway had many years of successful experience at National Cash Register, U. S. Steel, and Gillette, and could acquire clients easily. Three young fellows

– Alan Dohan, Bob Quirk, and I – were challenged to fulfill assignments meant for twice our number and double our experience level. We did this and grew like pine trees. I enjoyed everything about Executive General, especially providing criminal justice consulting services – psychological testing, program evaluation, institution audits, and human side of work training.

After a year, I learned there was a faculty position open at Northern Kentucky State College. I applied and was hired to teach economics, management and organization, and organizational behavior in 1970, the third most important year of my life. When I told Frank Steely, the president of the College, that I never had a course in economics, his response was, "You'll do fine – teach principles of economics by using Paul Samuelson's text, *Economics*." I added an excellent reader, *The Worldly Philosophers,* by Robert Heilbroner. Three years of teaching macro and microeconomics, principles of management, and organizational behavior were highly enjoyable. I viewed myself as a product of teachers, and the opportunity to teach others was enormously fulfilling. It was another good fit. **The lesson learned from Executive General and Northern Kentucky State College was to say yes to challenges. Just because you haven't done something doesn't mean you can't learn to do it. It can pay off to stretch yourself. Stimulation and growth are highly satisfying, and the rewards are great.**

In 1970, I had the security of a faculty position but needed additional money to raise a family. Teaching is a labor of love, but the income is low. Many professors do studies, write books, and give talks to make ends meet. I chose to consult one day a week when classes were in session and three days a week during the summer. I finished two projects with Executive General in 1970 and made two additional calls – one to the Sun Oil Company because I thought Exxon would have its consulting needs met; a second to King Kwik Markets because I thought Kroger would have its consulting needs met. Fifty-two more years of consulting came from word-of-mouth referrals beginning with these few clients. When you love what you do, word spreads.

From the beginning, I have followed two practices that have served me well: (1) Never do more than one-fourth of my projects with one client, industry, or profession. This has resulted in a steady flow of work, and my courses and consulting have been enriched by variety; (2) Every week, I do something for an old client, current client, and future client. This has kept me learning and growing and has resulted in deep loyalty with clients. I have met the one-fourth limit with clients in criminal justice, transportation, finance, manufacturing, retail, construction, education, and health care. When this happens, I refer clients to other qualified and trusted consultants. I continue to have consulting clients in multiple fields, but never more than one-fourth. This approach has kept my 'projects' pipeline full and has kept my classes interesting at the University. It's led to scholarships, internships, and first jobs for graduates.

I learned three important lessons from my clients in 1970.

1. I cared about morale and productivity in all workplaces, but I related especially to the social good that could be done in the field of corrections. I thought if I were just starting college, I would like to major in philosophy and psychology with a concentration in corrections. I also learned the importance of being flexible in providing consulting services. I was used to doing I/O tasks, conducting studies, and providing human side of work training, but a young and talented Commissioner of Corrections asked for one-on-one sessions once a month to brainstorm initiatives, sort out priorities, and talk through policies and personnel problems. **Lesson: coaching was a little-used term in the 1970s, but I learned how helpful it could be with this excellent leader.**

2. I prepared thoroughly for every client, picturing the process and expected activities, but as often as not there were still surprises. When a Sun Oil senior leader unexpectedly gave me a check before providing services, saying it was an expression of confidence, I said thank you and put the check in an escrow account until services were complete and satisfaction was declared. When executives were at a planning meeting in Florida and the Ohio River froze over, preventing the transportation of oil in the Midwest, the room cleared immediately, and people were on planes within an hour. **Lesson Learned: emergencies happen, and clients have mission-critical events that consultants must honor and help address.**

3. I learned that all clients are unique, and some could be candidates for the 'Most Memorable Person' feature in a Reader's Digest issue. Some became friends for life. Such a person was Sam Vinci at King Kwik Markets. Sam grew up in the Italian area of Cleveland, was full of mischief and testosterone, and played linebacker for the Cleveland Browns. He said the hardest thing he ever had to do was to TRY to tackle Jimmy Brown. He said it couldn't be done by one player and it usually took three. Sam had musical ability and could sing like John Belushi of the Blues brothers. To these characteristics, he added a heart of gold, the principles of a priest, and the curiosity and tenacity of a mountain goat. Sam was a great vice-president of Human Resources. **The lesson we learned was about the excellent work people could do together and how satisfying it could be for years and years.** Our projects included recruitment and selection, television training skits, behavior modification, management development, store staff training and cross-functional team

building. Sam and the King Kwik executive team made retail history in Cincinnati and the convenience store industry.

#11

Five Early Decisions That Proved to be Good

In 1973, I made five consulting decisions that proved to be good.

1. Deciding what I could do best and wanted to do most. When you have many interests, it can be as important to decide what not to do as it is to decide what to do. I had three choices:

> *a. Personnel selection/assessment*
> I understood tests and measures, psychological profiles, and employee surveys. My dissertation was *Predictors of Success for Million Dollar Round Table Members.* I found four predictors: 1. A life pattern of hard work; 2. A significant role model in insurance or a related field; 3. A current need for money; and 4. A positive and supportive relationship between the agent and his or her leader.
>
> *b. Labor relations*
> I worked intensely in Labor Relations for three years and

loved it. It was important work and I felt useful. The United Auto Workers (UAW) became an early client and with the American Federation of Labor and Congress of Industrial Organizations (AFL-CIO) spearheaded the development of an Associate Degree program in Union Leadership at Northern Kentucky University.

c. Training and development
On a philosophical level, I cared about the human condition. On a psychological level, I wanted to help people fulfill their potential. On an educational level, I related to learning and teaching. I chose training and development as the primary activities in my university and consulting work. A theory of vocational choice highlights the importance of early experience. Many years of camp counseling, youth leadership, and coaching sports helped prepare me for teaching and consulting.

2. Diversifying clients – having no more than 1/4 of my consulting projects and activities with one business, industry, or government organization was important. This kept my classes current and interesting and kept the pipeline of projects full. Example areas and clients are:

a. Criminal Justice – States of Ohio, Kentucky, Indiana, Pennsylvania, Florida, and Corrections Corporation of America

b. Transportation – American Public Transportation Association, Federal Aviation Administration, Airports Council International, and ATE Management Systems *c. Corporations* – American Electric Power, AT&T, Choice Hotels, Duke Energy, Great American Insurance, IBM, General Electric, Kroger, Marion Merrell Dow, and Marriott

d. Healthcare – American Medical Association, Johnson & Johnson, National Institutes of Health, Baptist, Catholic, Jewish, Methodist, and University Healthcare Systems

3. Specializing in 3 services and 8 areas of expertise. The services are 1. presentations (annual and national meetings – keynote and concurrent sessions), 2. organization development (planning, team building, and problem solving), and 3. professional/management education (seminars and coaching). Areas of expertise encompass the eight books in the *Human Side of Work series*: Morale, Performance, Ethics, Motivation, Stress, Communication, Group Dynamics, and Leadership. Train-the-trainer clients include the Association for Quality and Participation, the Commonwealth of Kentucky, and the United States Navy.

> For example, I provided a train the trainer program on stress management for the U.S. Navy at a world conference in Norfolk, Virginia in 2007. The title was *Life, Work, and the Pursuit of Balance for Professional Wellbeing.* Topics included: How to predict and extend life expectancy; the definition, causes, signs, and consequences of stress; the critical balance between the demands we face and our resources for coping; myths, realities, and strategies for dealing with change; personal and professional coping skills; the importance of attitude; and the five characteristics of a hardy personality. Subjects were made practical for individual and professional use.

I tailor the title and content of talks and seminars to the audience or group. Examples include Managing the Stress of Being a Lawyer; Physician Well-being – Handling the Frenzy, Frustration, and Fatigue; The Human Side of Engineering, Banking, Transportation, etc.; The Art of Caring Leadership for Company Success (AT&T, Duke, GE, Kroger, Marriott, etc.), and Ethics—Fire in a Dark World.

Clients often use *The Art of Leadership* text as coursewares focusing on topics and activities to meet the needs of the audience. Creative instructors add stories, cases, and examples to make the subjects relevant and useful. For example, I use the terms *traditional, participative,* and *individualistic* to describe different styles of interpersonal relations with the message to value differences as strengths and the prescription to be wise, caring, and flexible to meet the needs and gain the gifts of different kinds of people. A food or hospitality company may use analogous terms such as chocolate, vanilla, and strawberry; a science or engineering company may use the terms solids, liquids, and gases; an artistic or graphics company may use the terms dot, line, and squiggle. The message is the same – celebrate differences! Different types of sports, kinds of coaches, and styles of players can be used to enhance understanding of styles of interpersonal relations. Everyone learns better when the process is fun.

People enjoy learning about the styles of interpersonal relations of famous figures in history: Moses and Queen Victoria were *traditional*, known for their high standards and social order; Eleanor Roosevelt and Benjamin Franklin were *participative*, people-loving and people-serving; Joan of Arc and Henry David Thoreau were *individualistic* champions of freedom and following the beat of individual conscience. Winston Churchill had a versatile style – his love of the British Empire, devotion to the monarchy, and dedication to the rule of law were *traditional*; his love of family and robust interaction with friends all his life were *participative*; at his core, he was *individualistic*, self-defining and self-expressing to his last breath at age 91. His friend, General Lord Ismay summarizes Churchill as venerating tradition, loving people, and abhorring personal constraints and convention.

Valuing differences to achieve high performance was the message of a presentation I made at a national conference on aviation safety sponsored by the FAA, funded by Eastern Airlines, and conducted at Emory-Riddle University. The title was 'Aviation Safety: The importance of communication and the role of personality in the cockpit, control tower, and boardroom.' Participants learned the special contributions and leadership needs of: *traditionals* who ensure high standards, reliable structure, and clear organization; *participatives* who bring communications, teamwork, and smooth human relations; and *individualists* who add creativity, spontaneity, and innovation. The point was emphasized that where diversity exists, patience, understanding, and tolerance are needed. **The lesson: We are like crayons in a box – some are bright and shiny, some are soft and warm; some are used a lot, some are new and pointy; Together, we make a beautiful world. In any case, we all have to live in the same box.**

4. Using time management principles based on core values, yearly goals, and a daily "to-do" list; and *keeping* paperwork current and simple. Effective time management has been a performance multiplier and my number one stress management tool. By keeping records current and simple, I passed two IRS audits with ease.

5. Executing a daily work regimen – every working day, do something for an old client, something for a current client, or something for a prospective client. Examples are making a check-in call, sending a timely book or article, solving a problem, etc. This regimen has been appreciated by clients and has kept my days full of satisfying and meaningful work.

The Lessons I learned from these five decisions were the importance of clarity, balance, focus, organization, and discipline. None of the decisions came naturally to me, but the order they brought allowed me to be more creative, spontaneous, and much more effective as a professor and consultant.

#12

The Absolute Need to Live and Work by Five Core Principles for Consulting Success

What do clients want? They want a consulting service that is current and focused on the client's needs. They want competent, thorough, and timely work performed. They want the consultant to be suitably aggressive in serving their needs – not so slow that opportunities are missed, not so fast that mistakes are made. They want the consultant to tailor services to the client's best interest and outcome. In 1980, based on 10 years of consulting experience, I wrote a philosophy of consulting with 5 core principles. I called this five-finger consulting. These principles work for all consultants in all fields of endeavor. The principles are burned in my brain, and I follow them religiously:

1. *Always* focus on mission and values versus style and technique (putting client interest first).

2. *Always* tell the truth as you see it (with kindness).

3. *Always* keep job knowledge current (concepts and skills).

4. *Always* **plan and prepare thoroughly but remain flexible (whatever it takes).**

5. *Always* **deliver superior results (satisfaction guaranteed).**

The practical wisdom of number two is supported by Mark Twain who observed: If you always tell the truth, you won't have to remember anything. I think I remember that right, but in any case, it's the truth.

The world of work is filled with moral dilemmas, and the consultant is often in the thick of these – what to do about an unethical colleague or client, what standards and values to model and uphold, etc. Although human relations always involve compromises, your conscience should be your guide in matters of right and wrong. Philosopher Lou Marinoff states morality is an old idea that is more fundamental than legality. What is the consultant to do? Follow the dictum, "non harm to sentient beings." If an action causes harm to others, don't do it. Bad forces can be large and powerful; all the more reason to be a strong force for good. **In moral dilemmas, use your best thinking, listen to your heart, and let reason be your guide. Never knowingly do harm to others; and when in doubt, always do the loving thing.**

#13

The Importance of Questions

    Will Rogers had a way of conveying simple truths, saying that when you do all the talking, you only learn what you already know. In 1991, I learned the importance of asking questions, listening responsively, providing helpful information, and encouraging solutions that the client will implement. I was consulting with the Baptist Health Care System when the Technology Vice-president and I had a long dinner over the challenges and plans for his operation. I knew nothing about his area, but I was genuinely interested and curious to learn. I asked why something was the way it was and listened intently to the answer. I asked why the answer was the answer and listened to understand. I asked 'why' seven times until the root cause of the problem was revealed. I asked what the client was going to do and encouraged him to implement the solution. The client looked at me with appreciation and said, "You ask the best questions. You make me think about the answers and now I have a solution and a path forward."

    As a consultant, I learned the value of caring about the client, asking questions that require client thought, listening

carefully versus talking, and championing principle-based actions the client will take to solve the problem and advance the organization.

#14

How Teaching Helps Consulting and Vice-Versa

Courses taught and lessons learned:

a. **Economics** (growth through challenge)

Teaching economics was a growth experience for me. I had never had a course in economics when I was assigned to teach large classes of Macro and Microeconomics. The best way to understand a subject is to learn it well enough to teach it. The great thing about this was Paul Samuelson's textbook, *Economics*, now in its 19th edition. I taught out of the 10th and 11th editions and could well understand why he received the first Nobel prize in economics largely because of this seminal text. It was thorough, clear, understandable, and highly interesting. It was a masterpiece. I added a complementary reader, *The Worldly Philosophers*, by Robert Heilbroner. Students liked this book because it put a human face on economics, often called the dismal science. **Lesson learned: Teaching economics for three years helped me in my consulting work, most of which was for business clients.** I learned the concepts of scarcity, supply and demand, costs and benefits, incentives, efficiency, ownership, and purchasing power.

b. ***Management and Organization*** (learning the functions and settings)

Management and Organization was another course I had never taken in college. **What I learned by studying a good text provided a strong foundation for my work as a professor and consultant.** Management is planning, organizing, directing, and controlling the work of an enterprise. Without planning, there is confusion; without organization, there is inefficiency; without direction, there is drift; without control, there is waste. I taught the four functions of management by requiring students to understand and use these in a semester-long management project. Students were divided into groups (management teams) based on Allport, Vernon, and Lindzey's *Study of Values* assessment – theoretical, economic, religious, aesthetic, political, and social orientations. Each group learned management concepts, principles, and tools by applying them in planning, organizing, directing, and controlling a real-world project.

Examples: An economics group designed, produced, and sold NKU license plates and gave the proceeds to an orphanage; a social group conducted a career day for a youth club, including games and prizes, and helped each participant create a heroic journey story for his or her life; a political group managed the campaign of one of its members who was elected Mayor of Union, Kentucky; a theoretical group managed a project to increase the number of books in the Northern Kentucky University library; an aesthetic group managed a campus art and music show; a religious group managed a church carnival event for a building fund. In addition to mid-term and final exams over the text and class lectures, and individual term papers on management topics, the management team projects helped students 'learn by doing.' Theory must be put into practice for the best and most complete learning to occur.

c. *Behavior Theory and business practice* (the course I know best)

This is a course I knew well, based on theorists, such as Frederick Taylor, Elton Mayo, Kurt Lewin, Abraham Maslow, Douglas McGregor, William Menninger, Chris Argyris, Frederick Hertzberg, Rensis Likert, Saul Gellerman, Harry Levinson, Gordon Lippitt, Henry Mintzberg, George Odiorne, Peter Drucker, Robert Greenleaf, Edgar Schein, Warren Bennis, W. Edwards Deming, Ken Blanchard, James Collins, and others. When I think of each one, I think of a fundamental concept, principle, or tool he taught. I used a good Organization Behavior text and a reader on human behavior as the coursewares.

Every class was participative, practical, and personalized for the students. Subjects included work morale, productivity, leadership, motivation, communication, ethics, etc. This was a popular course with students because it bridged the gap between school and work. Many students continued their educations in Industrial/Organizational Psychology, Organization Development, and Business Administration. Others pursued careers in human resources and labor relations. Many found the course to be helpful in their roles as leaders. **Lesson: Teaching this course helped me stay current about human side of work subjects, both in the classroom and the consulting world.**

Sometimes an aspiring professional will say, "I don't have time to read the theorists in behavior theory and business practice." I ask them, do they want to be a six-cylinder car with only 4 cylinders working, or do they want to properly prepare and be an 8-cylinder engine, and provide the high performance that clients and students need? Too many consultants have little understanding of the history and philosophy of their field and are focused on tools, techniques, gimmicks, and fads without knowing their foundation and evolution. With some effort, this can be corrected.

d. *Small Business Management* (a creative course)

I started teaching this unique course in 1972. It was a challenge for me because I wasn't an experienced businessperson. I found a three-part solution: 1. The Small Business Administration had a not-for-credit course on how to own a business. The learning materials were outstanding. Each student did a feasibility study on owning a business. Examples include a bridal shop, funeral home, detective agency, accounting firm, and a moving company. The feasibility study included the Skeleton Key (legal structure and organization), the Golden Key (financial matters such as money required and where to obtain it), the Front Door Key (location and marketing), and the Master Key (management and staffing), etc. 2. I used a good text on Small Business Management for lectures and exams. 3. The high point of the course was a YPO (Young Presidents Organization) Panel at the conclusion of the course.

The Young Presidents Organization (YPO) members are individuals who are presidents of their own companies before the age of 45, with a required number of employees and required level of revenue. They lead highly successful manufacturing, retail, and service companies. Members belong to the organization until age 50. They are recognized as successful entrepreneurs in their communities across the U.S. and the world. There are more than 29,000 members in more than 130 countries. By the end of the course, a small percentage of students want to own a business, but all students have a thorough understanding of small business challenges and deep respect for any business owner. Five members conduct the two-hour YPO Question & Answer Panel for the class. The panel never ends on time. **I learned the generosity**

of most successful business owners; they genuinely care about young people and their development, and are more than happy to share their experience and advice.

e. T-Group Theory and Laboratory Method (a one-of-a-kind course)

When students look back on their college educations after 10, 20, or 30 years, this is the course they always remember. It's a highly experiential and interactive course where students learn how they affect other people, and also how others affect them, in an unstructured T (for Training) group lab. They learn what a healthy person is and what a healthy group is by being these in a group setting. Important sub-themes of group dynamics are addressed – empathy, interpersonal trust, mutual respect, hidden agendas, social perception, prejudice, personal attitude, non-verbal behavior, helpfulness and psychological safety. A book of readings on personal and interpersonal growth and a book report on human relationships, such as Carl Rogers' *On Becoming a Person*, complement the T-Group Lab. **I learned the importance of honesty in personal growth and interpersonal relations.**

f. Humanistic Psychology (the human potential for growth)

In 1982, I was asked to attend an American University course on teaching humanistic psychology in a university. Our Psychology Department was strong in the behavioral and psychoanalytic schools of psychology, but there was a gap in the area of 'growth' psychology focused on the human potential for personal and interpersonal development. Today, this is called Positive Psychology. A wonderful text by Duane Schultz is the backbone of the course. The theories and methods of personality psychologists are taught in a participative and personalized way, including Sigmund Freud,

Alfred Adler, Carl Jung, Erich Fromm, Karen Horney, Gordon Allport, Abraham Maslow, Carl Rogers, Erik Erikson, Viktor Frankl, and Fritz Perls. Psychoanalysis teaches the importance of early and subconscious determinants of behavior, the dynamic interplay of the id, ego, and superego, and the role of defense mechanisms. Behaviorism teaches the powerful paradigm of stimulus, response, and reinforcement to understand and shape behavior. Humanistic Psychology teaches the ways for fulfilling one's human potential. **Lesson learned: All three schools of psychology help us understand why people do what they do. It's immensely important for a consultant to have a fundamental understanding of the many facets of human thought and action.**

Learning the content and preparing to teach these courses in the university setting improved my effectiveness in the consulting world. I was current in research and theory. Consulting experiences helped me stay knowledgeable and stimulating in the classroom. Opportunities opened up for student field trips, internships, cooperative education assignments, scholarships, career counseling, and employment.

#15

Working Unfettered – Consulting Success and the Ghost in the Machine

For fifty years, Nancy was my ghost in the machine. She was a beautiful wife and mother who thought like a Pope. Her number one love was family, including our dogs, cats, horses, and every other critter. We met at a Cincinnati country club in January 1967 and were married two months later. I introduced myself as an Austrian ski instructor the night we met and clinched her attention by walking on my hands the next night (our first date). Nancy was a model in her youth and saw the world. For the next 50 years, her happiness was our family and being in the barn, woods, and field.

Nancy liked home life, so I kept work life separate, except to ask her advice for the talks I gave, and classes I taught. Subjects ranged from leadership to stress and her usual response was to ask, "What do you know about that?" I would say, "Not a lot, what do you think?" I always took notes and when the audience's attention faded, I would say, "Now, this is what Nancy thinks." Like magic, eyes looked up, people leaned forward, and pens were cocked. Nancy's 'thoughts' were always exactly right, and doable.

Her approach was like Beatrix Potter – the shorter, the simpler, the better – and the audience loved it. In 1990, Nancy had a serious stroke. At the bedside, Dr. Waller said, "There are some things that can't be explained," Nancy smiled, pointed upward, and said, "Yes, head of the animals."

I called Nancy every day when I was on consulting assignments. She was usually in the barn feeding someone and always had a story to tell me. I would tell her what restroom I used that trip to change from traveling clothes to a suit. We liked the thought that we were a team. Nancy loved our kids, all animals, and me. As for consulting, she was my wise and loving ghost in the machine. Success would have been impossible without her.

The lesson I learned is that no two people are exactly alike in their interests and temperaments, even if they are in love and share the same goals. She learned the wisdom of Benjamin Franklin's advice: Keep your eyes wide open before marriage and half shut afterward. I also learned the two best things in the world are the infinity of the universe and the intimacy of a close relationship.

#16

The Brain, the Terrain, and Creating Your Future – Ben Carson's Story

Lesson: Our lives are determined by what we tell ourselves, the people we are around, and the books we read, as the following story shows.

A few years ago, NKU invited Ben Carson, Director of Pediatric Neurosurgery at Johns Hopkins Hospital, to give a public lecture on life as he saw it, and the human potential for growth. He began by reminding the audience that we all have a brain, and he told us what the human brain could do. He didn't elaborate, but we got the message: We each have tremendous ability that we may or may not be using. He went on to say that he isn't a historian, but he believes there has never been a time or place in history where people have had more freedom to determine their own lives than they do in America today. Again, he didn't elaborate, but everyone thought, "Yes if I want to go to school, if I want to get married, if I want to have a child, if I want to move to Alaska, I can."

Then he said, "Let me tell you a story." He told us about growing up in a poor and dangerous part of Detroit. The projects were physically treacherous and psychologically numbing. He said that for the first eight years of his life, he never thought of himself as living long enough to become an adult. When he looked on the street, or in the hall, or at the TV, people were being killed, so he never expected to grow up. Also, he never thought of himself as a person because no one else seemed to. In fact, he felt no different than the couch or a lamp in the corner, certainly not someone of exceptional value. Then, two important things happened when he was nine years old.

First, his mother thought that books were important, so she required him and his brother to go to the library each week, pick out a book to read, and write a report for her. She would grade the report with a red pencil, while the boys told her what they had learned from the book. It was only much later in life that they learned their mother couldn't read. Through her attention to them and by reading books, they learned about Marco Polo and China, and dinosaurs, and many other wondrous things. The second event occurred when his fourth-grade science teacher put him in charge of the class rock collection and a lizard in a jar, as if he could do these assignments and was worthy of important responsibility. From this experience, Ben Carson developed respect for himself, and this served him well during his growing-up years. The path from 9 to 21 wasn't easy, and it wasn't always positive; but from the attention his mother gave him, the respect his teacher showed him, and the influence of books, Ben Carson made it through high school and college and was accepted into medical school.

There, he failed his first year. The Dean met with him and explained that not everyone was cut out for medicine; maybe he could pursue another career. "No," he said. "I'm committed to becoming a doctor." Then the Dean said, "Maybe you could go at a slower pace and have a less rigorous schedule." "No," he said. "Please let me take the same difficult path all doctors must take." When the Dean gave Ben a second chance, he dedicated his mind and every waking minute to the arduous task of completing medical school. As he told us, by combining the belief that he would be a doctor one day with the discipline of hard work, he achieved success. Ben Carson completed his medical training and was employed at Johns Hopkins Hospital in the Department of Pediatric Neurosurgery, where he led his colleagues in the first-ever successful separation of identical twins joined at the head.

The influence of people who cared about him, books that enriched him, and the belief that he was a worthy person were the factors that shaped his life. Then Dr. Carson went on, and he told the audience about reading another book, *Man's Search for Meaning*, by Viktor Frankl. The premise of this book is that every person needs a purpose in life, something important yet to be done. This made Ben Carson think about his own life and the purpose that would give it meaning going forward.

Dr. Carson remembered fourth grade and the importance of his mother, his teacher, and books. He thought about nine-year-olds and what most fourth graders want. The answer was prizes — ribbons, trophies, and stars, in other words, recognition. He knew most children received such prizes through athletics, and this was good, as they built their bodies and developed good character through sports. But he also thought, wouldn't it be good if children also received recognition for achievement in science? Indeed, it would be very good. In addition to his work in medicine and government, Ben Carson's purpose in life is to establish a science award for every fourth-grade classroom in America.

When Dr. Carson took his seat, each person in the audience was left to think about her own brain and her own opportunities, and the importance of her own associations, books, and self-concept to determine her life. Over the years, I've seen many presentations that could be called genius strokes. Morris Massey's "What you are is where you were when," Bob Caplon's "Day in the life of a leader," and Fred Young's "How to get rich and stay rich" are examples of such seminars. Steve Jobs at Stanford, J. K. Rowling at Harvard, William McRaven at the University of Texas, and Rick Rigsby at California Maritime Academy are examples of such commencement speeches. These have powerful and lasting messages. Ben Carson's talk is in that category. It has helped me help others fulfill their potential through positive self-talk, strong and caring relationships, and good books.

#17

Consulting Partnerships Where One and One is More than Two

I've had many enjoyable consulting partnerships, no two just alike, as the following examples show:

Kent Curtis. A Minister once asked me about Kent. Here is what I said: Kent's great strength is his teaching ability – the students love him because he loves them. A second strength is his leadership ability – he does the right thing, and he does it always. Kent's main strength is his nature – he accepts responsibility and puts the wellbeing of others first. Our friendship and affection grew with every passing year, from 1970 to the present. Kent's best pal is his dog, Benny. They make a good pair with morning and night walks at the dog park and long naps.

Kent excels at helping people fulfill their potential. In the years 1970 to 1990, he and I often consulted together. Kent brought a calm thoughtfulness to our projects and clients loved his deep values and unpretentious ways. Every consultant is unique in his or her own way (some would call it quirky), and Kent had an interesting habit. When we traveled to a client location, he always read the area's morning paper, cover to cover. He wasn't doing this to prepare for the client; he just enjoyed reading the paper and learning about what was going on in the area.

One time while serving a transportation client in Connecticut, we learned an important lesson. We were asked to conduct a two-day management retreat focusing on leading quality, including tools and methods. The first day went well, but at dinner the client asked us if we could change the focus of learning the next day. They valued quality management but thought team-building on the senior leadership team was a greater need. We had prepared for one subject, but another was needed. Without hesitating, we made the switch. The client appreciated our flexibility and felt thoroughly served. **Kent and I learned successful consulting requires listening to the client, keeping an open mind, focusing on the client's important and timely needs, and having the ability to change gears and direction quickly with no fuss.**

Mike Campbell. I don't have a one-word description for Mike. Three sentences are – 1. He was an old Kentucky philosopher who loved people and wrote poetry. 2. He loved Bonnie, his wife, three good daughters and sons-in-law, and they all loved Dad. 3. He was a vocational educator who understood the importance of career development and the role of caring teachers. Five more points: 1. When there was a power outage at Kentucky Power, Mike always had crackers and candy in his drawer. 2. Mike loved his church and taught Sunday school his entire adult life. 3. He was frugal and never wasted money, telling his leadership classes, don't take the books-we'll use them again! 4. He was an early adopter of technology, and made slides on Harvard Graphics that astounded his colleagues (How could an old geezer do that!?). 5. Mike's favorite project was the cabin he and Bonnie built in the woods by a stream. He wrote, "Everybody should be quiet near a little stream and listen."

Mike and I enjoyed philosophical discussions that sometimes led to use in leadership development. One day, we were planning a unit on resilience and adaptive capacity for young leaders. We were sitting next to a bubbling brook in a Kentucky State Park discussing the importance of a rubbing rock. We thought a smooth and small rock should be picked from a creek by the user and should be carried in one's pocket. If things got hard at work or tough at home, the rock should be rubbed till resentment, anger, and worry went away. Young leaders today enjoy finding a rubbing rock, and old leaders still use their well-worn friend. **Mike was a dear friend who taught me a fundamental consulting lesson: Good outcomes begin and end with good relationships, and these are based on mutual respect and trust built over time.**

Beverly Watts. Bev was born to be a community builder. She is a Black woman with the widest range of social skills I have ever seen. For over thirty years, I watched her devote her life to the well-being of others, first as Director of the Commission for Human Rights in Kentucky, then as Director of the Commission for Human Rights in Tennessee. She is patient, understanding, compassionate, wise, and courageous, and she uses these qualities every day from morning to night in service to others. The most 'political' group I have ever served as a consultant was a state commission for human rights, at one period of time. The Board Members were mostly middle-aged Black preachers who were charismatic, talented, and impactful servant leaders of their individual flocks; but together, they were ineffective, as each one vied for influence in the group. They simply wouldn't work together without Bev's calm and understanding leadership. They would be roaring lions until she helped them find a shared purpose and a constructive path to serve the entire community. Visibly and meaningfully, they turned into pussycats and became an effective board, as much as pussycats can be.

Bev once helped me provide a program on valuing diversity as a strength, for mass transit. It was a train-the-trainer program using the book *Building Community* as the courseware. Six pairs of trainers from the client organization learned the content and activities for three seminar-workshop days that they would teach to their peers in maintenance, operations, and the office. The plan was for me to teach the content with Bev's assistance and for her to coach the client training pairs in their deliveries. When she arrived in Cincinnati from Louisville the first morning, I had laryngitis and could not talk, so Bev taught the content and I assisted her. When she arrived in Cincinnati from Louisville the second morning, I still had no voice, so Bev taught the second day of content while I assisted. When she arrived from Louisville on the third morning, I still could not talk, so she taught the third day of content and I assisted. The unspoken message was powerful – Bev knew the subject and we were a team. The credibility of the diversity initiative and its value to the organization was enormous. It was recognized with a national award for diversity education. **There is usually more caught than taught, and most people go by the behaviors they see more than by the words they hear. The client saw the value of diversity through our example. We showed mutual respect, trust, and support through our actions. We were a team!**

Dan "drill down" Ronay. Dan could have a career in Hollywood playing a Marine Corps Sergeant Major. He has the physical presence of a marine and is the living embodiment of the military mantra – *mission first, people always*. In 1990, David Donahue, the Indiana Department of Corrections Commissioner, asked me to work with Dan to create a Department of Corrections experienced and emerging leadership development program. He said "Dan is simply the best educator I have ever known, and you will enjoy working with him." 'Enjoy' is an understatement, because working with Dan is like being in the front jeep of the Third Army in WW II. It's a 'learn, create, and serve-a-minute experience' one never forgets. Dan first studied Kentucky's Leadership Development initiative led by Commissioner John Rees, and tailored Indiana's to meet the needs of that state. The *Experienced and Emerging Leadership Development Program (EEL)* became a national model and is now in its 22nd year, spanning multiple Governors and Commissioners.

I've never been in the military, but working with Dan must be similar. One day, he dressed like General Patton and tailored his talk (with music) to the corrections audience. It brought smiles, then tears, then energy to explode the room, and created commitment to lead and serve. Dan was just being himself. Dan "drill down" Ronay is an outstanding leader and creative educator as the following story shows: An October Leadership Retreat with EELs included a Halloween skit contest with eight participant teams. The goal of each skit was to teach a timely and important leadership principle or practice. My role was to judge the presentations on content, delivery, and impact. I wore a black robe and used a courtroom gavel provided by the Dean of our Law College. EELs will never forget the camaraderie of the evening and the leadership lessons of the skits, thanks to Dan. **Consulting learning message: I started working with both the Kentucky Department of Corrections and the Indiana Department of Corrections in 1970. Every initiative requires establishing productive partnerships based on trust and shared commitments to be successful.**

Steve McMillen. Steve has an enormous ability to relate to every demographic – teens and grandparents, men and women, every race and ethnicity, every culture, every religious and political persuasion, and every sexual orientation. To Steve, they are all people and maybe he can help them. He has excelled as a leadership development and organizational effectiveness expert inside

4 large companies – Thomson Corporation, Hillenbrand Industries, O'Charley's Inc, and the Tennessee Valley Authority (TVA). Today, he is an outstanding external consultant in the areas of talent management, organizational development, and executive coaching. Steve's words are golden – if he says something, it's true; If he says he will do something, count on it! His greatest strength is his ability to help others grow and fulfill their potential. He is a natural-born coach and developer of people.

As a young academic advisor, Steve would close the door, put two chairs together, lean forward, and say, "I'm all ears." Students loved his casual style and the full attention he gave them. In the same manner, Steve is a superb executive coach today. When Kent Curtis and I asked Steve to be the third author on *The Art of Leadership* text, he declined, knowing he couldn't commit the time it would take. Steve's cup was full, and his priorities were straight. He knew when to say no . . . on both the first and second editions of the text. Regarding quirkiness, Steve loves sports of all sorts, especially high school and college football. Take him to any state in the country, and he will know the history of high school and college football in that state. Talk about an icebreaker! **The main thing one learns from Steve is congruence. He is intellectually and personally honest. He won't do something he thinks is wrong, and he will always do what he thinks is right.**

Joe Ohren. Joe was a role model for combining academic rigor with service learning, as his students studied and solved real-life problems. Students learned and the community was served. Joe was my first consulting partner, beginning in 1972. Our clients included local, state, and national government entities. We enjoyed working together immensely, especially conducting leadership and staff retreats for government agencies and commissions. Joe understood government, I understood psychology, and we both understood organization planning and development. I've never known anyone who knew his subject better, and this is what clients need from their consultants.

The one word that best describes Joe is expert. The second-best word that describes him is charismatic. He attracted bright and eager students and infected them with a love of public service. Joe developed Public Administration to be one of the most popular majors at Northern Kentucky University. Students learned under his influence, and his graduates have been working as public sector professionals for over 50 years based on his example. Joe will say it all started with his own mentor at Syracuse University, a professor who sparked a life-long commitment to public sector service.

Working with internal and external partners has increased my effectiveness as a consultant and has resulted in tremendous personal satisfaction. Each colleague has brought special knowledge and skills and working together has been thoroughly enjoyable. Most consultants will experience productive partnerships in their careers. Examples are:

- At AT&T, internal consultant Dave Sprouse was knowledgeable and deliberate, while I was current and fast. We helped AT&T in the area of organizational effectiveness for many years.

- At the University of Colorado Health System, Sue Wehrspann was experienced and wise and highly effective in leading change, while I could provide train-the-trainer consulting on coping with the stress of change.

- At IBM, Bob Caplon understood his company and was an A-1 performer, while I understood the human side of work and could teach the subject to IBM supervisors, managers, and executives. We worked together from Washington D.C.

to Hawaii, and one time Bob saved my life when, at an IBM reception, I leaned against a broken guard-rail of a Hudson River mansion rooftop. I would have fallen over 100 feet if he hadn't caught me. Now, that's a helpful partner.

- At Cianbro Industries, Alan Burton understood the history and culture of his company and was a discerning thinker. We provided leadership development as a team and still do. Alan's wisdom, concern for others, and integrity are unsurpassed.

- At Cardinal Hill, Kerry Gillihan focused on staff and leadership development to create the gold standard for rehabilitation medicine. Kerry was a servant leader and role model for caring leadership.

- In higher education, Charles Leffler, vice-president of North Carolina State University, and Gerald Hunter, vice-president of Norfolk State University, knew their institutions well and how we could work together to reinforce positive work cultures that support student learning.

- Steve Boyd knew communications and I knew leadership, as we worked together to serve IBM, P&G, Milacron, and the Kroger Company for many years.

- Ron Seal is a highly effective health care executive. We worked together for over 20 years in three healthcare systems, focusing on healthcare quality, patient satisfaction, staff morale, and leadership. Ron is a charismatic hospital executive and was featured as the best of the best in the Hurricane Katrina disaster. In 2017, he and his wife Marcia flew from Dallas to Cincinnati to be present for my right hip replacement at Christ Hospital. I felt 'covered' by Ron, Kent Curtis, and Steve McMillen as Patrick Kirk and his surgical team, great partners themselves, restored my mobility again.

- Chuck Holmes, Bret Scott, Al Linder, Jimmy Turner, John Rees, and Dave Donahue understood the world of corrections and worked with me intensely to improve leadership in the profession. Their impact has been enormous in prison management and correction reforms for nearly 50 years.

- Jim Youngquist and I have been allies in service to regional government leaders for over 40 years. It's safe to say that Jim is the Father of Regional Government Planning and Service Effectiveness in the Southeastern United States.

- Pete Jordan of Choice Hotels and Gordy Snyder of Commonwealth Hotels are Masters of Hospitality. We have worked together for 46 years to change the industry in the areas of guest satisfaction, staff teamwork, and leadership development. A short story: The Frisch's Big Boy statue (14 ft by 10 ft) disappeared one night. No one knew who took it or where it was. The Cincinnati Enquirer story, "Where's Big Boy?", sparked an enormous increase in sales in the Big Boy restaurant chain. It's never been discovered who hijacked Big Boy, and he was returned to his perch a fortnight later. It's hard not to have suspicions. Gordy Snyder and Pete Jordan are hard-working, fun-loving, and popular young executives who have led highly successful hospitality profit centers their entire careers. Like many leaders, they have an exuberance that makes work fun while advancing the enterprise. To this day, they both say they have no idea who took 'Big Boy.'

- Paul Quealy understood management education and the business needs of Milacron. We worked as a team to provide mid-management training in leadership ethics, including on-the-job applications.

- Mark Brooks is an exceptional educator who draws from rich experience as a leader in law enforcement and the U.S. military. He is younger and I'm older, so the exercise he taught me is especially fitting as it bridges generations. Mark advises young leaders to identify the person who has taught them the most about life – What was this person like? What lesson did they learn? The qualities of these real-life teachers and the lessons they taught are the inspiration and curriculum for leadership going forward. Talk about relevant, talk about buy-in, talk about effective... what an elegant exercise this is!

- Terri Bonar-Stewart and I served mass transit as a team for many years as she understood the needs and we worked together to tailor solutions for the industry. We worked together at Tastemaker, a Cincinnati flavors company, and worked together serving the Catholic Church and the City of Covington.

- Walt Lovenberg and I worked together at the National Institutes of Health (NIH) and in pharmaceutical companies to help science leaders in the areas of strategic planning, communication, teamwork, and performance management. Walt represents the perfect combination of caring about the work and caring about the people.

- Rob Followell knew hospital administration and I knew leadership development when we met. We worked together for over twenty years in 5 states and 4 hospital systems in the areas of leadership education and positive work culture. Rob has a keen mind, heart of gold, and winning personality. His approach is to work effectively with physicians and staff to achieve excellence in health care. I'll never forget the name of a band he formed with some West Virginia Doctors some years ago, *Bad Neighbors.* No matter how good they were as musicians, it was still probably better not to live next door.

- Dan Gregorie and I have worked together from 1992 onward to improve physician leadership in healthcare systems. Dan is captured in a snippet: He was scheduled to begin a talk to physician leaders when a hotel housekeeper asked him for help. She couldn't understand her medical bill. Body language told it all – the distraught woman looked confused and worried as Dan leaned forward to hear every word. With a reassuring smile, he told her what to do to solve the problem. The physician audience was important but could wait because there was a person who needed his help. I don't know a more principled, caring, and tenacious health care thought leader than Dan Gregorie.

- Jeff Walter and I worked together for over twenty years. We were a good inside-outside team to provide leadership development tailored to the Great American Insurance Company's needs. Jeff's strength was making sure we addressed real business needs in a usable way. He never wasted money and always put the interest of others first. Jeff was respected throughout his company and his services were always in demand. Jeff often provided training for the company's subsidiaries and partners in China. He was so well-liked and respected that they called him 'Teacher Jeff' and asked him to name their children.

Jeff and I were scheduled to conduct a leadership retreat for the American Financial Group/ Great American Insurance Company in Atlanta. At the pre-retreat dinner, we saw a handsome man rotating around the dinner tables shaking hands. He was a poster-perfect, black-patched U.S. Marine named Clebe McClary, who we thought was someone's son. Come to find out, he was the keynote speaker! More than that, his message was from the heart and life changing. His delivery was a combination of Lou Holtz and Norman Schwarzkopf! The audience's reaction was electric, with a standing ovation. He did an encore including questions and answers. Jeff and I were the last to leave the room. We looked at each other in a stunned state of worry. WHAT in the world were we going to do the next two days AFTER THAT? We had an important agenda for leadership and company development planned, but we were like the local band following the Mormon Tabernacle Choir or Freddie Mercury!

We were devastated when we went to our rooms. Then, I got an idea. I called Jeff and we asked the hotel to give us a black tablecloth and scissors. The next morning when we addressed the group, we turned around and put on our black patches. When we faced the audience, they loved it and laughed because they all empathized with us and knew our challenge. **The lessons we learned were the importance of humility, humor, and staying on task. The audience saw we were humble and could laugh at ourselves, and we were focused on meeting their needs.** I have never heard a more impactful talk than the one Clebe McClary gave us. It addressed the honor and responsibility of leadership. Clebe and his wife came to NKU and gave our students a similar talk. He was wonderful!

#18

The Asexual Consultant

In Indiana in 1969, I learned the importance of professionalism at all times. A well-known and highly competent I/O Psychologist provided outstanding service to the Indiana Department of Corrections executive staff during the day, only to lose the respect of all when he made sexual advances toward a client staff professional that evening. Trust and credibility were destroyed.

I conducted a management retreat for a corporate client and unexpectedly received a graphic sexual invitation from a young woman participant to join her in the Poconos. There was nothing to be done except ignore the request and hope she would not repeat this mistake in professional ethics.

I facilitated a planning retreat in Miami to create a computerized airline reservation system for international travel. I arrived a day early with the intention of preparing the syllabus for my course at the university. The client suggested that I go to the beach to do this, but didn't say it was a nude beach. I didn't stay, and didn't mention it the next day – better to leave sleeping dogs on the porch.

In Virginia, I conducted a 2-day staff development program for a transportation client. When I returned to the hotel after dinner, I found a sexual proposal 'letter' that was beyond belief in detail and safety concerns. It required a police report and investigation.

Lesson: a consultant must live by the highest standards of moral conduct. This is especially true in two areas – human relations and financial matters. Simply stated, sex and consulting don't mix, and financial trust is a paramount value. It's an old label, but 'straight arrow' says this well.

#19

My List of Mosts

My list of 'mosts' include most challenging assignments, most physical group, most dangerous clients, most beautiful locations, most unusual story, and most appreciative audience.

a. Most challenging assignments – NIH/UAW/Teamsters

In consulting, current projects almost always lead to future projects, usually in unpredictable ways. In 1979, I gave the keynote talk for the National Association of Real Estate License Law Officials in Washington, D.C. The subject was Real Estate Ethics – moral dilemmas, levels of morality, and core values for real estate professionals. I used the high standards of Stella Wilhelm of the West Shell Agency in Cincinnati in the sale of our home and purchase of a new home as a case study. It was the perfect way to teach the subject. Rick Wolfe, who owned a real estate company in Washington D.C., asked me to give a similar talk to his agents. Rick's strong assistant Marge was married to Walt Lovenberg, a senior research scientist at NIH.

NIH. Walt Lovenberg thought a seminar on the 'Human Side of Science' would be valuable for the senior scientists of NIH. The subjects were Leadership, Psychological Size, and 2-way Communication. Resistance was voiced when the audience learned the seminar would address the importance of communication and the role of personality in research. If they were going to attend a 'psychology' seminar, where was B.F. Skinner and who is George Manning? The reception was cool until participants discussed how subordinates may fail to speak their minds or hesitate to report unpopular data because of the psychological bigness of senior science leaders. Two-way communication is needed, and this can be achieved best by showing respect for others through effective listening.

The message was: Better communication leads to better work relations which leads to better research, and this begins with leaders who use and don't abuse the psychological size coming from their position, reputation, and behavior. Position and reputation are good, but the behavior required is to raise the psychological size of subordinates through respectful listening. **At NIH, I learned the importance of being sure the audience understands a subject before entertaining questions. Within the first minute of my talk, a contentious hand was raised. I forged forward another minute to fully communicate my message. The dialogue that followed was great.**

UAW. I knew the United Auto Workers well as a Ford Motor Company labor representative, 1967-1969. I understood the value of the union and the power it possessed to bring good to the workplace. I understood the history of the UAW and its challenges as an organized labor union. I also knew the tremendous social skills of their elected leaders at the plant, regional, and headquarter levels; these were intelligent and street-smart people who had risen to positions of great influence. When I was asked to provide leadership development for UAW's international leaders in 1974, it was a great honor . . . and challenge. The challenge was overcoming the participant mindset that I had been a company labor representative, taught psychology, and was very young. It worked out well, thank goodness, and led to much good. Participants agreed on three points: 1. Regional leaders need to spend more time in the plants interacting with front-line members; 2. Regional leaders need to understand and address the needs of all union members, in addition to a vocal few; and 3. Union and company management must work together to achieve a high morale-high performance work environment.

Efforts to improve the quality of work performed and the quality of work-life experienced should be shared by labor and management. This is documented in the Sharonville Story, a successful 'quality of work-quality of work-life' partnership that changed the work culture and saved a plant. Another outcome was working with Bill LeMaster and a committee of UAW and AFL-CIO labor leaders to create an Associate Degree Program in Labor Studies at Northern Kentucky University. **The lesson I learned was that labor and management leaders can take the low road of a power struggle that can destroy a company or take the high road of working together to create lasting success. Which path is taken depends on the goodwill and practices of the leaders on both sides of the table. Labor and management agreement on core values and supporting actions is the strength of an organization. A trusted third party can be helpful in facilitating this agreement and taking productive action steps.**

Teamsters. I was conducting an employee development program – The Human Side of Transit – in Tucson in 1980. This was during a period of conflict between the International Brotherhood of Teamsters and company management. The program focused on employee teamwork and passenger relations. A night of truck lights in the motel window, honking horns in the parking lot, and threatening phone calls led to police intervention. A calm and courteous meeting the next morning between union and management leaders resulted in understanding and joint support of a shared goal – employee training. **Lesson: This experience showed me how important it is to involve people in matters that affect them. If management and the union had discussed the employee development program before implementing it, confusion and conflict would have been avoided.**

b. Most physical group – Kentucky Cabinet for Human Resources

In 1983, I provided consulting services for the Kentucky Human Resources Cabinet, beginning with a retreat for Cabinet Secretary Al Austin, a beloved and charismatic leader who looked like Sir Walter Raleigh and wrote poetry like Lord Byron. Governor Martha Layne Collins relied heavily upon Al, partly because his Cabinet was so large and impacted so many citizens' lives. She also depended heavily upon Gordon Duke, Secretary of the Kentucky Cabinet for Finance and Administration, because this cabinet supports the work of all other units of government. Gordon was a role model for understanding government and achieving results. Al and Gordon were examples of experienced, dedicated, and highly effective public servants.

Al's Commissioners and Directors of social insurance, family service, public health, mental health, and workforce development agencies were picked for experience, competence, and commitment. As a group, they had more enthusiasm and physical energy than any group I have ever served. It was thoroughly noticeable when I met them in a retreat setting. I was physically fit, but it was everything I could do to keep up with their pace and volume of work.

A little-known story about Kentucky Governor Martha Layne Collins, the first woman to hold the office, and the only one to date, shows the importance of effective leadership. In 1983, she had a goal to convince Toyota to choose Kentucky as the location for the company's U.S. Headquarters and largest manufacturing facility. The Japanese selection committee arrived late in Kentucky because other states detained them far past the agreed-upon schedule. The Governor would not leave the airport until her guests arrived. The competing states lost points with the Japanese delegation because they made them late. Kentucky gained points because the Governor would not go home until she welcomed them personally.

The following day included tours and talks including Kentucky memorabilia of horses and bourbon. This went well, but the clincher came after dinner on the porch of the Governor's home in Frankfort. Unbeknown to anyone, including the Cabinet and staff, she had arranged with the Capitol Police to provide a magnificent fireworks show over Frankfort in honor of her Japanese guests. The Japanese visitors loved the fireworks! The next morning the agreement was made to establish Toyota's North American Headquarters in Kentucky and build Toyota's largest manufacturing plant in Georgetown, Kentucky.

From Al Austin's Human Resources Cabinet, I learned how the physical energy, enthusiasm, competence, and commitment of leaders can stimulate the performance of government personnel to a level fully as great as the private sector. From Governor Martha Layne Collins, I learned the importance of knowing your customer, and the importance of keeping secrets till the timing is right.

c. Most dangerous clients – razor blades and buttons

Two unusual experiences stick with me – one in corrections and the other in mental health. (1) I stayed on-site during a two-day evaluation of a minimum-security prison in Kentucky. While taking a shower, I found a razor blade embedded in the bar of soap. (2) During a tour of a mental health hospital in preparation for a leadership seminar, I met a button-eater, a resident who was fixated on swallowing buttons, including the buttons on the collar of my dress shirt. I was in and out of many correctional and mental health facilities over the years, especially during the 70s and 80s. When Nancy read Truman Capote's book, *In Cold Blood*, she insisted that we obtain an unlisted telephone number. **The lesson: personal safety is important. Don't assume it's a given in any circumstances. Make sure to stay safe. And that lost button you've been wondering about? I may know a guy.**

d. Most beautiful locations

As a consultant, I gave speeches, seminars, and workshops in many places for many years – church basements, art museums, universities, government and corporate conference centers, public libraries, courthouses, factory floors, and a riverboat. What matters is the service and result, not the location; but some settings are strikingly beautiful. For example: Airports Council International – Key West; National Food Association – Colorado; IBM – Hawaii; Marriott – Palm Springs; Hilliard Lyons – Phoenix; International Rendering Association – Bermuda; and Marion Merrell Dow – France and Italy. **Consulting lesson: there is no correlation between location and results. Enjoy the beauty of great locations, but work hard for the results.**

e. Most unusual story – Boris, Dino, and the $3,000 suit.

This story fits the theme of this book – *never a dull moment, oh my!* In 2001, I was asked to give an opening morning talk for the annual meeting of the International Association of Convention and Visitors Bureaus in Vancouver, Canada, following the Tribal Chief of the Assembly of First Nations in Canada. It's a long flight from Cincinnati, so I wore comfortable clothes on the plane. After passing through customs, I learned my luggage was lost. I immediately flagged a cab and asked the driver to take me to the nearest Department Store as fast as possible to buy needed dress clothes. When I explained the situation, Boris the driver said, "No problem. I can fix this!" Boris wanted to immigrate to America from Russia, but only made it to Canada where he had many friends, including Dino, the best tailor in Vancouver. He said Dino was a master Italian tailor and he had the best suits in Vancouver. I was desperate, so off we went to Dino's.

Dino measured me and said he would send the suit, tie, shirt, belt, and shoes to my hotel room by 5:00 pm. Sure enough, Boris arrived on time with everything – including the most continental-looking and feeling outfit one could imagine. It was glorious, but it looked like my homeland was Sicily. This was an international conference, so I fit right in. But the suit was not an American model from Penny's or Macy's, and it cost $3,000 at the time. Anything that wasn't silk was alligator. The next afternoon, after a pleasant evening and successful morning opening speech, I told my host what had happened. He said, "Please don't worry – we've spent more than that on the table flowers. Please accept this as a thank you gift from us to you." **What did I learn? Expect the unexpected, truth is stranger than fiction, allies like Boris and Dino are important; keep dress clothes with you on the plane, and Italian suits have more silk and sheen than a woman's dress. Twenty-one years later, I wore the same lizard suit and alligator shoes when I gave away my granddaughter Jessie in marriage. It was still sheik, silky, and shiny.**

f. Most appreciative group – Beverly Enterprises Nursing Homes.

Since 1977, I've addressed many audiences on the topic of stress, including law enforcement, aviation, radio stations, public utilities, transportation, hospitals, physician groups, law firms, financial companies, manufacturers, etc. The most appreciative audience I've ever had was the nursing home administrators of Beverly Enterprises, the largest Nursing Home Company in America at the time. The nursing home administrators requested the subject of stress management for professional resilience. I was honored to speak and prepared a program tailored to managing the stress of being a nursing home administrator. I don't know a more stressful environment than a nursing home, and I don't know a more stressful position than owning or managing a nursing home. There is a never-ending cascade of problems to prevent and resolve – resident health, family relations, staff training, maintenance and housekeeping, buildings and grounds, technology, financial and budget matters, food and nutrition, government regulations, and inevitable physical and social emergencies.

The lights were off, I was on stage, and the audience was large as I talked about the signs, causes, and consequences of stress, and discussed tried and true coping skills. I personalized the subject and could feel the appreciation of the audience in the dark. It was a deeply moving experience for me. Years later, Nancy was in a nursing home several times. I was thankful for the understanding and accommodation of administrators to let me stay overnight many of those times. **What did I learn? When you spend a night in a nursing home, you soon become like staff, and you learn firsthand how important, satisfying, and *demanding* this meaningful work is. There are many people who work in caregiving positions, who deserve the deepest respect and greatest appreciation society can give. This lesson applies beyond nursing homes and hospitals. When possible, go on site where the client lives and works and get firsthand experience – restaurant kitchen, police cruiser, building site, fishing boat, etc. Then you can truly speak to their condition and experience.**

#20

Large Scale Consulting

Large scale consulting projects can extend over a period of years. Examples include: 1. The Commonwealth of Kentucky; 2. Federal Aviation Administration; 3. Marion Merrell Dow; 4. American Electric Power; 5. Corrections Corporation of America (CoreCivic); 6. Cardinal Hill Hospital; 7. Health Alliance and Tri Health; and 8. Clermont County.

a. Kentucky Government (3 pivotal projects)

In 1983, I conducted a Cabinet retreat for the Governor of Kentucky, Martha Layne Collins. At that time, Kentucky Governors could serve only one four-year term. Governor Collins knew the importance of having a compelling vision, three clear goals, and an effective execution strategy for the eight members of her Cabinet. Her Secretaries were individually strong, but she knew they must work effectively together for the next four years. I had conducted similar planning and team-building retreats with her two principal assistants – Mary Helen Miller for the Kentucky Legislative Research Commission, and George Russell for the fifteen Area Development Boards of Kentucky. The Cabinet retreat was conducted at Kentucky Dam Village. I remember getting out of a helicopter in bright sunlight and entering a dark lodge where the Cabinet members were assembled. I couldn't see anything for five minutes, as we launched immediately into a highly participative two days of work together.

Agreement on direction and principles of conduct were the results of the retreat that guided the group for four years. Their three unifying goals were securing Toyota's North American Headquarters and largest production plant in Kentucky, establishing a Delta Airlines Hub at the Northern Kentucky/Cincinnati Airport, and making highly visible and productive 'service' visits to every county in Kentucky, taking government to the people. During the following four years, each Cabinet Secretary and Commissioner had a similar retreat tailored to the needs and goals of his or her area of responsibility – Finance, Transportation, Revenue, Justice, Energy, Human Services, Corrections, Natural Resources, etc.

The Governor's Cabinet worked intentionally to be a high-performance group. They assessed themselves on the characteristics of an effective group, capitalizing on strengths, and addressing low spots in the following areas: Clear mission, informal atmosphere, lots of discussion, active listening, trust and openness, disagreement is OK, criticism is issue-oriented, consensus is the norm, effective leadership, clarity of assignments, shared values, and personal commitment. The group took the time to build mutual respect and interpersonal trust. They worked effectively as a productive team for four years in service to the people of Kentucky. **Lesson learned: Martha Layne Collins showed how a caring and committed leader can assemble a team and achieve enormous success by having a vision with clear goals and creating a positive work culture, in government.**

Understanding the importance of vision for personal, organizational, and societal success is due greatly to the works of Peter Drucker, Jim Collins, and futurist Joel Barker, among others. A positive vision focuses and energizes people. Adding hard work and commitment, modeled and reinforced by leaders, makes a powerful formula that can overcome lack of resources and other handicaps and adversities. Peter Drucker explains the importance of vision: Because the modern organization is composed of specialists, each with her or his own narrow area of expertise, its overarching purpose must be crystal clear. The organization must be single-minded, or its members will become confused. They will each define "results" in terms of their own specialty, and impose its values on the larger organization. Only a focused and shared vision will hold an organization together and enable it to produce. Without agreement on purpose and values, the organization will soon lose credibility and, with it, its ability to attract the very people it needs to perform. Helping clients develop a grand plan that is 1. Leader-initiated, 2. Shared and supported, 3. Comprehensive and detailed, and 4. Uplifting and inspiring is highly meaningful and very enjoyable consulting work.

b. FAA (Generals, the planning imperative, and meeting rules)

From 1975 to 1995, I worked with many aviation organizations including the Cincinnati, Cleveland, Denver, Dulles, Indianapolis, Lehigh Valley, and Washington D.C. airports, the Airports Council International, the American Association of Airline Executives, LifeNet-Air Methods, and Embry-Riddle Aeronautical University. In 1994, I was asked to facilitate the development of a grand plan for the nation's airports (excluding military). Senior leaders of the FAA were charged with creating a document that would guide airport construction and development till 2050. These were the best individuals to do this in terms of knowledge, expertise, and responsibility. What was helpful in this two-year effort was when the group early on agreed-upon seven rules for meetings: Start and stop on time, one person talks at a time, every idea is given a hearing, honesty is the best policy, listen to understand, stay on task, and give your best efforts. The FAA airport-planning product was excellent. The meeting rules the group created are often used by planning groups and project teams to produce good results. **Lesson learned: spend time when a study or action group first forms to agree on goals and norms of behavior.**

c. Marion Merrell Dow (stiff in Strasbourg)

When Walt Lovenberg was appointed Head of Research for Marion Merrell Dow in 1987, he understood the need for agreement on direction and an execution strategy that would result in world-class drug discovery and development. He knew the company's scientists and their leaders were strong individually and he wanted them to work together to create a vision, mission, goals, initiatives, values, and culture document that would guide and support Marion Merrell Dow research facilities across three countries – Italy, France, and U.S. Walt asked me to work with him and his leadership team to facilitate planning and team-building efforts. The resulting "grand plan" was a success because it was homegrown, developed in a highly collegial way, and implemented effectively. Results were tracked and rewards were provided that reinforced both effort and accomplishment.

I enjoyed working with Walt and his scientists for five years. The people were great, the mission was meaningful, the locations were beautiful, and the customs were charming. A particular custom that challenged me was experienced in Strasbourg, France. There is so much wine! One night after too much dinner and way too much alcohol, I went to bed, and noticed that my body was totally stiff. I was so stiff that I couldn't move. I actually wondered if I would wake up in the morning. **I learned four lessons working with Walt: honest, thoughtful, and decisive leadership works well across cultures; collaboration across labs and disciplines boosts morale; when leaders model and support goodwill, performance rises to extraordinary levels; Europeans drink a lot of wine.**

d. Kentucky Power and AEP today (senior leaders get what they want and will work for)

As President of Kentucky Power, Dick Boyle sponsored four years of leadership training for every Kentucky Power supervisor, manager, and executive. The *Human Side of Work* series (eight books in a box) was used as coursewares for this leadership development initiative – two subjects each year. The initiative was: 1. Owned and worked at the top with active participation by the senior leadership staff; 2. Sustained over time versus a one-time-only flash in the pan activity; 3. Deemed strategically important to achieving Kentucky Power's critical success factors – safety, power, efficiency, cost, workforce development, and area economic growth; and 4. Based on behavior emphasizing on the job application of effective leadership principles and practices.

When Dick was promoted to AEP's senior executive staff, he mentored Brian Tierney in caring leadership. Brian put into practice the principles of servant leadership throughout the company – access (being available), communication (listening effectively), and support (providing guidance and resources). Employee morale and company performance flourished. **Lesson learned: Leaders can be obstacles to creating a positive work climate, or if they are the kind of people who want a healthy work culture, they can usually have it. They may have to work hard for it, and it will take time and resources, but if leaders desire to achieve a positive and healthy human environment, it can be done under**

almost any circumstances. My role was to be a sounding board and encourager to the leaders of Kentucky Power and AEP beginning in 1990.

Dick Boyle's success with AEP and Kentucky Power calls to mind another leader. Sam Walton, founder of Walmart, was a leadership role-model for caring about people. He was America's richest person when he died, and he was beloved by all who knew him. Why? He showed up for work on Saturdays because his employees did. He remembered employees' birthdays and anniversaries because they were important to him. He had donuts on the dock to talk about problems and possums because he enjoyed it. He drove an old truck and never put on airs. He said, take my inventory, take my buildings, take my money, but don't take my people. He knew he could lose the first three, but if he had his people, he could get it all back. Sam Walton's prescription for success was to *care about people*.

e. CCA (the leadership pyramid)

CoreCivic, formerly Corrections Corporation of America, owns and manages over 100 private prison and detention facilities with 14,000 employees and almost $2 billion in revenue. In 1999, the company began a multi-year effort to develop effective leadership practices throughout the organization. The initiative was conceived and implemented by the senior executives of the company, principally operations president Jimmy Turner. My role was to provide train-the-trainer leadership education based on the *Human Side of Work* series. I would conduct training for the senior leaders and directors, who presented the same training for wardens; directors and wardens conducted the same training for assistant wardens and captains; assistant wardens and captains gave the same training for correctional officers and first-line personnel – the people at the 'doing' level of containment and treatment.

CCA didn't farm out this training. They knew a common core of principles and practices and a pipeline of emerging leaders could be developed best if operations management carried the message while human resources and training personnel provided coordination and administrative support.

At the completion of the two-year initiative, Jimmy told a story about a company that had achieved greatness in its industry. The company erected a large billboard and painted the words: We Are Number One! As the years went by, the company neglected the policies and practices that had made them number one, and they neglected the sign as well. Weather erased a letter each year until the only words left were **We Are Numb**. Jimmy would not let CCA be numb, and he knew the solution was excellent leadership through continuous learning. **The message I learned from this is the importance of active and well-conceived involvement of senior leaders developing mid and front-line leaders and personnel in a company. Otherwise, time, attention, and resources are poorly spent.**

f. *Cardinal Hill Rehabilitation Hospital (leadership and the nifty fifty)*

Cardinal Hill Hospital in Lexington, Kentucky is one of fifty benchmark rehabilitation hospitals in the U.S. and is a strategic partner with the Easter Seals nonprofit organization. The success of the hospital is traced to good leadership. Kerry Gillihan succeeded Lyman Ginger, a respected and highly effective leader of the hospital for many years. Kerry built on this foundation and created the gold standard for rehabilitation care in the United States. Kerry was a servant leader and role model for caring about people. Kerry's leadership team worked as a team to focus, energize, empower, and support all hospital staff members to exceed the hopes and expectations of patients and their families. The spirit of a hospital can be ignited by senior leaders, who support middle leaders, who support first-line leaders, who support the front-line staff, who do 80 percent of the work.

You can tell when you enter a healing place – it shows in the countenance of people, and it shows in the healing touch of caregivers. It shows in the behavior of employees – are they fully present and professional in their actions? Do they teach each other and behave as a team? Do they put patient care first and foremost in all they do? Cardinal Hill is an exemplary rehabilitation hospital traced to excellent leadership practices. My role was to help the leadership team create a culture of caring over a period of 16 years. **What I learned in working with Cardinal Hill is the importance of trust and respect among leadership team members at all levels of responsibility. Time was taken to build team spirit at annual retreats with the leadership staff at Carnahan House, Spindletop, and Shaker Village. This included lectures, group discussion, and study-action projects to improve the organization. Equal time was taken with all staff members to permeate the hospital with a one-team attitude in service to patients.**

g. The Health Alliance and Tri Health (building community and building culture)

The Health Alliance was a Greater Cincinnati healthcare system comprised of University Hospital, Christ Hospital, Jewish Hospital, St Luke Hospital, and Hamilton Hospital. Tri Health was a Cincinnati area healthcare system comprised of Good Samaritan Hospital and Bethesda Hospitals. Both organizations were challenged to marry the diverse cultures of strong and long-established hospitals. The Health Alliance initiative was called *building community*. The Tri Health initiative was called *building culture*. Both hospital groups provided three seminar-workshop days for mixed groups of 40 supervisors, managers, and executives (800

Health Alliance participants and 400 Tri Health participants). The seminar workshops were spread over a period of six months and included three themes – Communication and Teamwork, Caring Leadership, and Helping People through Change. Each seminar workshop was sponsored by two Hospital presidents and included extensive question and answer sessions with the CEO, COO, and CFO of the system.

My role was to conduct these seminar workshops in a highly participative way, so information could be shared, new relationships could be developed, and participants could help their staff members adjust to new structures, tasks, technologies, and people. Eight hundred Leaders in the Health Alliance and four hundred leaders in Tri Health were asked to be role models for front-line employees in maintaining communication and teamwork, coping effectively with change, and providing excellent patient healthcare. Two enormous marriages of nine legendary institutions were achieved by excellent senior, mid-level, and front-line leaders. **Lesson learned – follow seven steps in leading change: have a good reason for making change; involve the people who will be impacted by change; go slow enough so people can adjust; keep people informed through unambiguous and constant communication; provide training in new knowledge and skill to support change; wait patiently for results; and acknowledge and reward people for adapting to change.**

h. *Clermont County (In the Interest of Children)*

In 1993, a three-year multi-agency effort was initiated to create a shared vision and action plan to work effectively at the 'doing' level to serve the children of Clermont County, Ohio. This was a joint effort of the Department of Human Services and the Juvenile Court of Clermont County, Ohio. The goal was to ensure the physical, social, and mental well-being of every child in the county.

It was conceived, sponsored, and paid for by the Clermont County Board of Commissioners. **I learned the importance of combining political will, administrative leadership, and professional support across the complete spectrum of government entities to achieve success. When leaders and front-line personnel have a shared goal and work together cooperatively to achieve it, the result can be magnificent. I learned wisdom is knowing what to do, virtue is doing it and this takes work**. Many people know what to do but lack gumption and grit to do it. Success was achieved by caring professionals working together 'in the interest of children' in Clermont County. My role was to facilitate this work with Clermont County leaders—Steve Brooks, Doug Brothers, Dave Clark, Martha Dorsey, Steve Wharton, and Stephanie Wyler—as an external consultant.

#21

Number One Consulting Skill – Time Management

In 1969, Bill Holloway taught me the fundamental principles of time management. I have used time management principles based on core values, yearly goals, and a daily "to-do" list, keeping paperwork simple, ever since that time. I would rate this as an essential consulting skill and coping technique. Checking off completed items on a prioritized 'to do' list based on your values and aligned with your goals is tremendously satisfying and a powerful reinforcement of productive behavior.

In 1975, I met John McCollister at a Fixed Base Aviation Management conference where we both gave talks. I've never known a more multi-faceted person – Aviation Dean, Lutheran Pastor, author of 24 books on baseball, National Anthem singer for the Detroit Tigers and the Minnesota Twins, pitcher for the Baltimore Orioles, and a wonderful speaker. John gave me a gift of the following words which have been inspirational and aspirational for me:

A master in the art of living draws no sharp distinction between work and play, labor and leisure, mind and body, education and recreation. He hardly knows which is which. He simply pursues his vision through whatever he is doing and leaves others to determine whether he is working or playing. To himself, he always seems to be doing both.

Nothing says who we are more than how we spend our time. Since 1969, I have followed the advice of the consultant's consultant, Benjamin Franklin:

Take Time
Take time to *think*,
it is the source of power.
Take time to *play*,
it is the secret of youth.
Take time to *read*,
it is the basis of knowledge.
Take time to *love*,
it is the essence of life.
Take time for *friends*,
it is the road to happiness.
Take time to *laugh*,
it is the music of the soul.
Take time to *give*,
it is too short to be selfish.
Take time to *work*.
it is the price of success.

Effective time management is the number one productivity and stress management skill of a successful consultant. Nina Tassi identifies Seven Key Traits of people who are at ease with time:

1. They never seem to be in a hurry. Even their body language is graceful and purposeful, not jerky and rushed.

2. They experience the present to the fullest, having the capacity to focus on the moment at hand, both in work and in play.

3. They take time to preserve their physical health, emotional well-being, and—importantly—their creative resources.

4. They set priorities and then work the list, which allows them to accomplish more than most other people.

5. They learn from experience and never harbor guilt, regret, or blame.

6. They spend time on relationships. They love to teach and learn from others as well as care and be cared for.

7. They live value-based lives, making sure their actions support what is truly important to them.

Consultant's lesson: using time management principles have made me twice as productive and half as stressed as I would be without this job aid for life and work.

#22

The Stabilus Story – Cross Cultural Communication and Business Success, Including the SPOT (Superior Products on Time) Manifesto

The most effective leaders have an integrative approach. They integrate different cultures, races, genders, and personalities into a whole that is greater than the sum of its parts. The integration is not a melting-down process; rather, it's a building up in which the identity of the individual is preserved yet simultaneously transcended.

Founded in 1934, Stabilus is a worldwide producer of hydro-pneumatic adjustment elements with 10 plants in 10 countries on 5 continents. Stabilus gas springs are used extensively, especially by automobile and furniture manufacturers. In 2000, CEO Dave Richeson invited me to work with Stabilus in the areas of communication, teamwork, and leadership development at its North Carolina location. The uniqueness of the company was its mix of German owners, Japanese customers, Mexican suppliers, and American workers. There is no question that different cultures have different customs and norms of behavior. Without losing the special attributes and gifts of the variety of national groups, the company flourished by valuing cultural differences as strengths while coalescing and living by core values of honesty, respect for others, service to others, and excellence in products and processes.

Human side of work training sessions were conducted for all front-line employees, first-level supervisors, mid-level managers, and senior executives. Stabilus employees created a **SPOT** Manifesto that became the agreed-upon performance standard for the company – **S**uperior **P**roducts **O**n **T**ime. A stuffed dog named SPOT became the symbol and cherished reward for fulfilling the spirit of SPOT. The stuffed dog SPOT was an earned reward, and everyone wanted one for her or his office or home. SPOT became an iconic Stabilus figure like the Chessie Railroad System's sleeping kitten Chessie.

Lesson: most international companies (German, French, Italian, English, Japanese, Swedish, American, etc.) value the perspectives and talents of different cultures, but the ultimate and final decision-making is the responsibility of owners.

#23

Train the Trainer Initiatives

The following are sample organizations I have served with 'Train the Trainer' initiatives: 1. AT&T; 2. IRS; 3. Kentucky Criminal Justice; 4. Kroger Company; 5. Queen City Metro; 6. Marriott; and 7. IBM.

a. AT&T – Mandated Restructuring

In 1982, AT&T was required to restructure the company. This involved over 200,000 employees who would be reconfigured into AT&T Long Lines and seven Baby Bells in 1984 – Bell South, Bell Atlantic, NYNEX, American Information Technologies, Southwestern Bell, US West, and Pacific Telesis. The challenge of change was enormous and so was the stress. I was asked to provide Train-the-Trainer workshops on 'managing the stress of change' for AT&T education and medical professionals during this tumultuous period. **Lesson: It's essential to work with the client to be sure the training content and delivery are tailored to the needs of the audience. My preparation included in-depth discussion** and planning with AT&T health and wellness, human resources, training and development, and operations leaders.

b. IRS – Helping People through Change

From 1985 to 1987, I provided Train-the-Trainer seminars on 'coping with change' for the Internal Revenue Service. In an effort to reduce bureaucracy and improve service, President Ronald Reagan initiated a 50% reduction of supervisors, managers, and executives in the IRS. This required many leaders to return to non-supervisory 'doing' jobs. Helping people move from states of denial, resistance, and a negative attitude to states of exploration, responsibility, and commitment was the goal. Coping techniques were taught including 1. Moderation. 2. Time management. 3. Sharing the load. 4. Learning when to say no. 5. Escaping for a while. 6. Decompression. 7. Talking with others. 8. Being less critical. 9. Managing emotions. 10. Slowing down. 11. Helping others. 12. Handling hassles effectively. 13. Having a hobby. 14. Celebrating the positive. 15. Developing job skills. 16. Trusting in time. **Lesson: Adjusting to change is challenging. Leaders can make the difference between positive and negative outcomes by modeling and reinforcing effective coping skills.** True-life IRS examples were used to make this point.

c. Criminal Justice in Kentucky – The Human Side of Work.

When the *Human Side of Work* 8-volume series was published in 1988, Bob Stone of Eastern Kentucky University sponsored a train the trainer week for EKU faculty in the three divisions of law enforcement, corrections, and courts. This was an honor and a highly enjoyable project for me. EKU now has a College of Justice, Safety, and Military Science and uses *The Art of Leadership* as the text for leadership courses. **Lesson: The contents of *The Human***

Side of Work series are mixed, matched, and tailored by faculty to meet the needs of the audience.

d. Kroger Company – Management Development, Building Community, and Training Effectiveness

Lesson: Good companies hunger for ways to keep their employees well-trained. The Kroger Company is the United States' largest supermarket chain by revenue with over 465,000 employees. Since 1981, I've had the opportunity to work with Kroger in the areas of leadership and professional development. The first project was coordinated by Human Resources Vice-President Paul Gibson. 'Executive Pairs' was a day-long workshop devoted to communication and teamwork in the executive offices of the company. Senior leaders often supported training initiatives for other groups in the company but had never had a development day tailored to improving the communication effectiveness of senior executives and their assistants, as well as teamwork in the entire executive office.

Beginning in 1988, all grocery store managers have attended a week-long course on the human side of management before assuming duties. This was developed by the Corporate Training Department led by Dennis Barton after completing a Train the Trainer course on the *Human Side of Work* series. Education principles and training skills have been taught to all company trainers including television recording and coaching, sponsored by Jim McLaughlin. The human side of engineering was provided to help Kroger maintenance and construction professionals deal effectively with people, sponsored by Phil Lewis. Steve Houchin sponsored company-wide management training on valuing diversity as a strength. John Wagner conducted a three-day Train-the-Trainer program for all Kroger human resources personnel, focused on the role of human resources in creating a positive work culture in every division and area of the company. The *Building Community* book was the courseware for this initiative.

According to the American Society of Training and Development, the overall U.S. commitment to training is 2.34 percent of payroll ($1,208 per learner), with more enlightened employers providing substantially more – from 2.5 to 5 percent of payroll. Truly great companies commit 10 percent of payroll costs to employee training. Training employees in soft skills significantly improves individual performance and increases employee retention, providing over 200 percent return on the financial investment companies make.

e. Queen City Metro – *Valuing Diversity in The Workplace*

Beginning 1974 and for over 30 years, champions of employee morale and organization performance at Queen City Metro were General Managers Ed Harvey – organization development, Tony Kouneski – leadership development, Mike Setzer – employee training, and Paul Jablonski – diversity education. 'Valuing Diversity as a Strength' was a two-year Train-the-Trainer initiative that received national recognition from both the American Public Transportation Association (APTA) and the Society for Human Resource Management (SHRM). This was because of the efforts of Terri Bonar-Stewart, Don Bennett, Vaughn Davis, Michael Washington, and Beverly Watts. All Queen City Metro employees from operations, maintenance, and the office participated in this popular human side of work initiative. **Lessons: The most senior leaders must understand, want, and visibly support a training initiative for maximum success; also, the consultant and company professionals must have believability and passion for the subject.**

f. Marriott – Quality Improvement through the Team Concept

During the 1980s, employee involvement to improve quality was a dominant business and government focus. I worked with many organizations providing 'human side of quality' training to complement the technical aspects of quality management addressed by W. Edwards Deming, Joseph Juran, Phillip Crosby, and others. In 1982, Roy Raskin asked me to provide Train-the-Trainer education on quality circles for the Marriott Corporation. They called the initiative *Quality Round Tables*. The initiative was successful because it was understood and supported at the top of the organization. Senior executives thought employee participation and problem-solving were in line with J. W. Marriott's belief that if management takes care of the associates, the associates will take care of the guests, and the guests will come back again and again. **Lesson learned: human resource initiatives work well when they fit the organization's culture and priority needs.**

g. IBM – Participative Management Primer

Beginning in 1982, I've had the opportunity to work with IBM in the areas of management education and coaching at over 20 locations from New York to California. For many years, IBM required every manager in the company to have 40 hours of in-service education each year, 32 hours of which had to be on people-building subjects such as communication, motivation, and leadership. At separate times, I was asked to provide Train-the-Trainer education on two required subjects – Business Ethics and Participative Management. The Business Ethics course featured moral dilemmas, levels of morality, adherence to IBM's three core values (respect, service, excellence), the nature of integrity, and the importance of courage. Every IBM manager whose name was on any government contract anywhere in the world was required to take this course.

The Participative Management course featured employee empowerment, group dynamics, and problem solving through the team concept. IBM thought the path of quality had boulders and pebbles. It took the strength of management to remove the boulders, and it took the involvement and commitment of frontline employees to remove the pebbles. All IBM managers were required to take the Participative Management Primer course. **Lesson: IBM believed effective management was necessary for company success, and that education would keep managers stimulated and growing throughout their careers. Even managers with more than forty years of experience were expected to attend 40 hours of education every year to keep them fresh and current.**

#24

Going Hollywood – Sara Lee, Dolly Parton, and the Stress of Change (Summer in the Dark Room)

In 1985, I was invited to speak at the Annual Meeting of Kahn's Sara Lee. The themes of the meeting were change in the food industry, leading change, and professional coping skills. I followed the Megatrends organization that reported on social change and its impact on food producers, including Kahn's Sara Lee. I was preparing to speak on leading change and professional coping skills when I noticed a high level of commotion behind the stage. What I saw reminded me of a Dolly Parton concert. I thought if there was ever a group that could benefit from stress management, it would be an entertainment or public events production company. A week later, Dan Gibbons of Audio-Visual Network asked me if I would conduct a seminar series on stress management for his employees. An additional goal was to videotape these seminars to produce four educational videos that would be distributed by the Association for Quality and Participation.

Working with Dan was immensely enjoyable, and the employees loved the four seminar workshops on managing stress. The unexpected challenge was the time it took to edit these tapes for accurate content and smooth delivery. Hours of tedious attention were required to be sure the subject matter was error-free and the media quality was appealing to users. The final product was distributed widely and was popular with the 6,000 members of AQP. But that summer editing videotape in the darkroom almost killed me. **The lesson I learned was that the time and skill needed to create good media is enormous . . . but worth it. The other message was the enjoyment of working with talented people sharing a common cause.**

#25

Most Stressful Groups

No one gets through life stress-free and in every person's life some rain will fall. Sample occupations that are especially pressure-filled, conflict-ridden, and frustrating include: 1. Physicians; 2. Attorneys; 3. City managers; 4. Chief financial officers; and 5. Emergency first responders.

1. Physicians – Handling the Frenzy, Frustration, and Fatigue

I've had the opportunity to provide stress management education for many physician groups – university faculty, hospital staff, specialty groups, and the American Medical Association. *An American Sickness* by Elisabeth Rosenthal helps explain why physician stress is so high. Erich Fromm said sick societies make people sick; it's also true that sick healthcare systems can make people sick. Physicians and other health care professionals are in the thick of this swamp with little personal ability to change the system.

Of all the audiences I have had, the group that stands out as the most 'developed' is Family Physicians. As a group, they are skilled, wise, and dedicated to the well-being of others. These individuals, too, are challenged to cope with stress in their lives. Many are helped by a strong ally, such as a partner at home or at work. The Greeks said a kite won't fly without a string, and a string won't fly without a kite; together, a kite and a string will soar. This analogy holds true for anyone living a demanding life. It takes at least two people who care completely and are *all in* for any endeavor to endure.

A physician once asked me if I thought he should retire. It's a case-by-case decision, but I shared this message: **There are three markers of a good retirement: physical fitness, social connectedness, and sufficient income. There are two inoculators against a bad retirement: someone to love and something important to do. There is a one-sentence recipe for a successful retirement: Move your body, open your mind, follow your heart, and count your blessings.**

2. Attorneys – Managing the Stress of Being a Lawyer

Beginning in 2001, I provided a seminar on 'Managing the Stress of Being a Lawyer' for Kentucky lawyers within the first year after passing the Bar Exam. A Kentucky Bar Association caravan goes to the various parts of the state to provide education – Louisville, Frankfort, Lexington, etc. Stress is physical and emotional wear and tear on the organism coming from pressure, conflict, and frustration. Like a metal bridge that wears down with weather and time, people 'age' from the problems in their lives, caused by others or caused by one's self. For the average person, half the source of stress is work and half is home and family. 'Managing the Stress of Being a Lawyer' focuses on both professional and personal stress, with special attention to avoiding addictions. An important goal is to live a balanced life at a healthy pace. **The lesson is: Every day do something for your physical, social, spiritual, and occupational wellbeing, and view life as a marathon, not a sprint.**

Remember, the happiest people don't have the best of everything, they make the best of everything they have.

3. City Managers – Building Your Personal Infrastructure

In 2004, I made a speech in San Diego on 'building your personal infrastructure' for the International City/County Management Association. David Krings was the President of the organization that year and performed one of the best 'think on your feet' acts I've ever seen. He was addressing the 1000-plus participants in the opening session when he lost his place in his notes. When he couldn't quickly recover, he was unflappable as he told the audience to just talk among themselves till he found his place. The audience loved it. David was a popular leader because he was humble and honest, and that's the nature of so many people who become city managers and county executives. As a group, they are responsible problem-solvers who care about the communities they serve. Dave is an Eagle Scout, and this doesn't surprise me. Richard Florida made a talk at that conference that has stuck with me: the 'place' that has three Ts is the one that will survive and thrive – talent (including good schools), technology (including infrastructure), and tolerance (so that everyone wants to live there). The task of leaders in public, private, and not-for-profit organizations and communities is to help create such places. This is a task that is meaningful, demanding, and can be stressful.

Professor Carl Stenberg of the University of North Carolina at Chapel Hill School of Government leads the Public Executive Leadership Academy that has served North Carolina for more than 15 years. As a faculty member of PELA, my subject is 'Building Your Personal Infrastructure – serving others and living to tell about it.' In 2009, I gave a talk on this subject for the Illinois City and County Managers Association. During a change of planes in Detroit, there was a scene being filmed for George Clooney's movie *Up in The Air*, so everyone in the concourse was asked to act normally and not watch the action as George rode the escalator from one gate to another. When the director called 'cut,' I called Barry Burton, host of the Illinois conference, and told him I was in a movie so the fee for my talk went up. There was silence at the other end. **Lesson: A good consultant has a sense of humor!** George Clooney is an alum of the theater program at NKU, although he was never in a course with me. Although we've never met, I'm told people often get us confused, which is understandable, since whenever anyone in a crowded place yells "George!" we're both likely to turn around.

4. CFOs – Post Enron Stress Disorder (the secrets we know)

In 2003, I had a seminar in Chicago on 'Managing Stress' for CFOs in the private sector. Manufacturing, retail, and service companies representing a wide range of sizes attended. Body language at the reception showed these individuals were under tremendous pressure, often had to deal with conflict, and were frustrated, as well. I featured the five characteristics of a hardy personality – commitment, control, attitude, perspective, and positive relationships – and personalized the talk for CFOs. The best part of the evening was the spontaneous questions, answers, and the helpful discussion that occurred. The discussion was intense and helpful. **A lesson learned: Some people are stress carriers. If a leader doesn't understand, appreciate, and support employees, stress levels go up. If they don't perform their own work well, causing problems for others, stress goes higher. If they don't do their own work right and things go wrong and they blame it on others, they are stress carriers. The CFO group resolved to do good work, show tangible support for others, and model and reinforce the five characteristics of a hardy personality.**

5. Angel calvary – Life Flight Stress

I've had the opportunity to provide stress education for air rescue helicopter crews in Kentucky, Georgia, and Florida. I don't know a job classification with higher morale than these flight nurses, pilots, and mechanics. The combination of working at peak performance, operating as a team, and saving lives in dangerous situations results in tremendous pride and satisfaction, also stress. Distress occurs if a life is lost or if crew safety is in peril. Distress can also occur in human relationships, especially when intense emotions are raised. Flirtatious and aggressive behavior can occur. Both love and hate can develop in these conditions. **Lesson: leaders must keep standards of behavior high, including zero tolerance for bullying and inappropriate sexual language or conduct.**

In dealing with stress, perspective is important. In this regard, Reinhold Niebuhr taught the following:

Give us the serenity to accept what cannot be changed, Give us the courage to change what should be changed, And give us the wisdom to know the difference between the two. This short maxim is tremendously helpful in stressful times and situations.

#26

What I Didn't Know That I Wish I Did Know

Experience is a teacher as three stories show—the red bus trip, the manager's hidden agenda, and the gun and knife show.

a. The Red Bus Trip

Some young consultants are wise beyond their years. I wasn't in this category as the red bus story shows. In 1973, Joe Ohren and I were hired to facilitate a planning retreat with the Board members and senior staff of a regional planning agency. Joe knew government history, issues, laws, and challenges better than anyone I have ever known. This was one of the first public sector projects that we did together over the course of many years. If I asked Joe to help me with General Motors or P & G, he would say, "No, I'm busy." But if I called the next minute and said the police department or water district or county roads or a state office or a federal agency needs something, Joe would always say, "Yes, how can I help?"

The leader of the organization we were serving asked us to bring the alcohol (beer, wine, liquor) to a Board retreat location, a

Kentucky State Park in a 'dry' county. We said yes, loaded my Red VW bus with refreshments, and headed for the event. We looked at each other, and both of us said, "Should we be doing this?" We realized the leader of the organization had asked us to do something we shouldn't be doing, because: We needed clear minds on the subject matter of the retreat to do good work; and someone could drink too much, misbehave, and have an accident. **Lessons learned: Don't be the one who provides alcohol at a public sector event, and be wary of unusual requests clients may make.** This client was a great public servant his entire career, and he, too, learned a lesson as a young leader. Young leaders have tremendous energy and creativity, but they may make a mistake if they don't think things through thoroughly.

b. *The Manager's 'Hidden Agenda"*

In 1983, I had a business retreat with a major U.S. corporation. The senior leader was competent, charismatic, and performing on all 8 cylinders. He asked me to facilitate an executive retreat to answer three questions: 1. Where are we now? 2. Where should we go? 3. How should we get there? What I didn't know was his romantic interest in a strong direct report. I later learned that many others did know, and the retreat was viewed as a relationship opportunity for the two of them, versus a business meeting. I listened to the senior leader sort through options going forward. He wisely chose to take a different position in the company. His organization was well served, and he married the direct report the following year. **Lessons learned: People are human; and it's important to keep reporting and love relationships separate, ladies and gentlemen must always treat each other as such, and honesty is the best policy. A good approach in the intake interview with prospective clients is to ask – Is there anything**

I should know that may affect the audience's receptivity to you or me or this event?

c. Gun and Knife Show, Sunday Morning Church, Ku Klux Klan, and The Kentucky State University Board of Regents

All is well that ends well, but a lesson was learned when four unique groups showed up at the same location on a Sunday morning. My group was the Board of Regents of Kentucky State University, a historically black institution. The other groups were a gun and knife show, Sunday morning church, and the Ku Klux Klan. The demographics of the four groups were vastly different. Imagine everyone's surprise when participants of all the groups climbed the steps to a community porch and common front door at 8:00 in the morning. The location was a large building in the country, and each group occupied a different area, so there was no formal interaction. Participants said they were glad it was a 'day' event and one of the groups was a church. **The consulting lesson: check the location and schedule of venues carefully.**

#27

Be Prepared – The Motto of a Good Scout (The Importance of Knowing a Day in the Life of the Client)

No two clients are alike. Different industries, professions, and organizations have different personalities and challenges. Examples of organizations I have served and know first-hand include courts, radio/TV, air rescue, prisons, universities, the Army, the Navy, builders, insurance companies, hotels, law firms, manufacturers, airports, transit organizations, churches, banks, medical practices, realtors, science labs, retail stores, hospitals, schools, and police. **Lesson: It helps to spend time learning the 'work' of the client. Site visits, interviews and observations provide important context.**

a. Bluegrass Foods – (watching sausage being made)

This is more interesting than one might think. Based on a strong German influence in the Cincinnati area, good pork products have been a food staple since the mid-1800s. Located in the Northern Kentucky area, Bluegrass Foods was an established part of this tradition. When the owners, Bill, Glen, and Jay Rice, asked me in 1989 to work with them in the areas of planning, organizing, directing, and controlling the business, I was honored. It was important to understand how the products were made, packaged, sold, and delivered, as well as bottlenecks and frictions in the company. Several days of preparation made me twice as effective as a consultant.

b. Independent Anesthesiologists – (miracles a minute)

In 1995, I worked with Phillip Bridenbaugh and his faculty at the University of Cincinnati Medical College in the areas of determining workloads, conducting performance reviews, and establishing reward criteria. Phil was the senior department chair in the medical college and the president of the American Society of Anesthesiologists. Dick Park was a graduate of the department and had created a large Anesthesiology practice at St Elizabeth Hospital in Northern Kentucky. To prepare for a planning retreat with the thirty-five physicians and staff in 1995, I spent a day in the life of an anesthesiologist. When I arrived early in the morning at the surgical center, I was impressed beyond words to see row after row of patients awaiting surgery. It was like a large garage with bays of cars or an aircraft carrier with planes lined up on the flight deck. I saw many medical miracles performed that day and was thankful in a deeper way for great doctors, nurses, and healthcare professionals.

c. Cincinnati Children's Hospital – (an Artist at work)

I began working with Cincinnati Children's Hospital in 1999. It's an academic pediatric acute care hospital providing world-class medical care for children since 1884. In preparation for a series of leadership retreats with the physicians and staff, I spent the night shift with Joe Luria of the Emergency Department. Joe is the epitome of physician excellence in dealing with children and their parents in medical crises. First, he knew what to do clinically with every child; second, he knew how to calm and assist every parent in the emergency department. Watching Joe and the medical staff that night was like watching Michelangelo paint. They were healers in the truest sense of the word. Our work together included seminars on the human side of healthcare and agreement on a patient care promise. Implementing these reinforced the high morale and high-performance culture of Cincinnati Children's Hospital, traced to the support of leaders Mike Buncher, Richard Ruddy, and Jim Anderson.

d. Pre-program profiles – (The Jack Eversole lesson)

In 1977, Jack Eversole, Director of the Barren River Area Development District, asked me to work with his staff in the areas of agreement on direction, having a healthy work climate, and maintaining professionalism in all matters. Jack was a long-time newspaper reporter and radio personality before assuming his leadership role in regional government. He could have also been a clinical psychologist, because he provided me with a one-page profile on every staff member, leader, and himself in preparation for working together. The profile described the cardinal disposition (example - optimist), central tendency (example - needs structure), secondary trait (example - loves sports), special talent (example - writes well), personal interest (example - girl scouts), and developmental need (example - computer skills) for each person. This preparation helped me work with Jack's staff in highly effective ways and is an example of doing the homework to achieve the best results. What happens before you're in the room helps what happens in the room to be much better.

#28

The Consultant Image – The Eye of the Beholder

The first time I gave my consulting image serious thought was in 1982. It was at a sales management meeting in Charlotte, North Carolina. My topic was the 'secrets of the cookie kid,' including a Walt Disney presentation on the seven practices of Markita Andrews, who has sold more Girl Scout cookies than anyone in the history of scouting. I matched this with customer-focused selling to make a popular and useful opening talk.

When coordinator Greg Whalen, an NKU business and marketing graduate, met me at the airport, he looked concerned and said, "We need to do something about that." I was carrying my lecture materials in a cardboard box; I called it my 'teacher box.' It functioned well because I could carry everything I needed with me from class to class and client to client. Greg said, "This is not a good image." He bought me a black leather carrying case that looked professional and gave me a tutorial about first impressions, including clothing and shoes. It's true that first impressions can become lasting impressions, so be aware of your image and put your best foot forward.

Greg advised me to dress to communicate the importance of the client to me, and to convey the image of a serious and seasoned professional. He said I should dress conservatively and neatly with quality clothes and shined shoes. Every teacher needs a teacher, and I took his words to heart. I always dress at the same level or more formally than the client: work slacks and sweater, versus jeans and sweatshirt; dress slacks and sport coat, versus work slacks and sweater; suit and tie, versus dress slacks and sport coat. Dress styles change over time; be a late adopter. But on the other hand, if you're still wearing huge lapels and ultra wide ties from decades ago, I can introduce you to Greg.

When traveling, keep business clothes in your carry-on luggage. I learned this lesson the hard way. I arrived late in New York City to do a management talk the next morning on 'leading across cultures' at IBM in White Plains. My luggage was lost, including a suit, white shirt, tie, and shoes. In the limousine ride to White Plains, two Wendy's executives said I would be the first person in history to give an IBM talk in jeans and a pullover. It was fun to hear about Clara Peller's famous question, "Where's the beef?", in Wendy's popular commercial. Of course, my own question was "Where's the suit?"

During a morning break, I switched into a suit and tie to the relief of everyone. The IBM leaders were understanding, but much trouble could have been avoided if I had kept my business clothes with me. **The lesson: dress appropriately to communicate respect and professionalism and be prepared for emergencies by keeping your business clothes with you.** IBM's famous dress code was relaxed in Hawaii, when women could wear a Hawaiian dress and men could wear a Hawaiian shirt.

When I think about a consultant's image, I remember what Thomas Edison said: *Light travels faster than sound. That is why some people appear bright . . .. before they speak.* Also, I think about the impact of people like Mother Teresa and Abraham Lincoln, who were known for their character. I think as well about the profound and helpful speeches I have heard from individuals with unimposing figures and clothes. This reinforces my belief that what matters most is the content, not the package. The client cares about the quality of the consultant's service more than the cost of the consultant's suit. And yet, when we show professionalism and respect in our attire, that sends a positive message.

A word about voice: I was giving a talk on 'Leading Quality' for IBM in Washington D.C. Mid-morning, a fellow in the back of the room became animated, leaned forward, and listened intently for the rest of the day. I looked forward to talking with him when he came to the podium at the close of the program. He said, "When you began speaking this morning, I thought I had heard your voice before. Then, it hit me – you sound just like Roger Rabbit!" I didn't know who Roger Rabbit was, because the movie was released just that week. When I saw the film and heard Roger talk, I thought, "My gosh, this is awful." A voice like Orson Welles' is a great gift, and one like Roger Rabbit's is no help at all. **Lesson: There are some things you just can't change, such as your basic voice and other physical features. In consulting, these are overshadowed by content and character. Although image is important, like beauty, it's skin deep. More important is what you know, how you act, and your thorough commitment to serve the best interests of your client. I think even Roger Rabbit would agree.**

#29

Reality and Humble Pie

How do you change others? The consultant must remember that you don't change others, they change themselves – and then only if you, by example, are a way they want to be, or if you teach knowledge and skills they choose to use. It's a rule: people do what they want when you are not there. Consultants can learn what Gandhi learned from his wife, Kasturba, during 57 years of marriage. When they were newly married, he would tell her what to do. He was full of strong opinions and recommendations. Her usual approach was to listen and smile, but then to proceed with her own methods and at her own pace. From Kasturba, he learned a lifelong human relations message – most people, in the final analysis, will do what they personally choose to do when you're not present. **Lesson: although consultants can and often do influence clients, the most effective consultants strive to guide and facilitate versus command and control.**

#30

Be a Continuous Learner
(Every Teacher Needs a Teacher)

In 1923 the Irish poet William Butler Yeats won the Nobel Prize in literature. He wrote, "Education is not the filling of a pail, but the lighting of a fire." I've had many great teachers, but five stand out: Arthur Steinhaus in physiology, Edward Mowatt in philosophy, Viktor Frankl in psychology, Lucien Cohen in psychology, and William Stewart in leadership. These professors were firelighters for so many people. They changed me because they loved their subjects and took an interest in my development.

There are four secrets to effective teaching and consulting. *The first* is to love the subject. From Accounting to Zoology, all good teachers and consultants do. They arouse love of the subject in the learner, making them believe what they are learning is important and worth sacrifice. *The second* secret is to care about the learner or client. This can't be faked and will be picked up without words. The essence of teaching and consulting is a positive relationship. *The third* secret is to provide knowledge or an example that the learner or client can use. Great teachers and consultants are experts in their subject areas and focus in on the most useful knowledge for the audience or class at hand. *The fourth* secret is to capitalize on teachable moments. This is important because the learner must be ready to learn.

John Dewey said education is what remains after the lessons have been forgotten. I don't remember the lectures Bill Stewart gave us in his Saturday morning classes; he rambled a lot and wasn't well-organized. But I do remember the principles he taught: **1. Focus on others, put their interests first; 2. Be a team player, teach others the rides; 3. Be professional in conduct and try your best.** This 'education' has helped me as a professor and consultant in ways untold for 52 years. Bill taught in threes because he heard storytellers say people remember three things best – three pigs, three bears, three blind mice, three stooges, three musketeers, and three act plays.

Lesson learned: The successful consultant must be a continuous learner and every teacher needs a teacher. The following colleagues have kept me stimulated and growing in their areas of expertise: 1. Leadership; 2. Teams; 3. Quality; 4. Vision; 5. Stress; 6. Ethics; and 7. Technology.

Walter Ulmer has forgotten more about **leadership** than I will ever learn. When I wonder if I have a topic conceived right and conveying what is important, I ask Walter. He provides context and color that give the subject life. From decision-making to discipline, Walter teaches leadership by example, drawing on his roles in military leadership and at the Center for Creative Leadership.

For 40 years, Steve Martin has taught me about **teams**, including the characteristics of an effective group, positive versus negative group member roles, how to develop trust and respect in a group, the role of the leader, and organizational interventions to create a positive work culture with special attention to psychological safety and ethical behavior. Steve embodies caring about people.

Professor of management Bill Lindsay thoroughly understands the **quality** imperative in the world of work. We wrote a

Participative Management Primer together and authored articles on quality improvement methods and processes for the Association of Quality & Participation. Bill has been an important thought leader in the global quality movement and has kept me current since 1980.

The role of **vision** in organizational life has been promoted by many theorists, including Peter Drucker, Joel Barker, and Jim Collins. They have taught the importance of having a positive vision of the future that will focus and energize behavior. They have shown how this applies to children, nations, and organizations. Beginning in 1993, Terri Bonar-Stewart has kept me current on this subject. I've used her thoughts and guidance in transportation, medicine, manufacturing, and even the Catholic church.

I didn't realize the impact of **stress** in the areas of morale and performance until Steve McMillen shared a paper and lecture on executive health by Hans Selye in 1980. The book, *Stress: Living and working in a Changing World* is now in its third edition largely because of Steve's influence. Steve keeps me current on the subject as we've served clients from NIH, AMA, Johnson & Johnson, and the U.S. military.

Ethics is the most important subject in the human side of work. Philosophy professors Jerry Richards and Joe Petrick helped me understand moral dilemmas, levels of morality, the role of values, the importance of courage, the dark side of leadership, and the need for leadership integrity. These concepts have grounded my consulting activities for more than 40 years.

My biggest professional challenge is without a doubt **technology**. From an ability standpoint, numbers are not a strong suit, mechanical devices shut me down, and buttons and dials are downers. Although I value and benefit from scientific achievements, I thoroughly relate to Albert Einstein's statement – *I fear the day will come when technology will surpass human interaction … the world will have a generation of idiots.* I think Henry David

Thoreau's admonition – *Beware, don't become tools of your tools* – has never been more important.

Because of the foregoing and the fact that I'm a professor and consultant, I have needed the help of many competent, caring, and patient people to function in the e-world, i-world, and cyber-world. Without the help of others such as Sarah Mann, Evan Downing, Jeff Chesnut, Bill Attenweiler, Susan Wehrspann, Jennifer Futrell, Kevin Warren, Lindsey Walker, Miranda Kinney, and Barb Thomes, I simply couldn't do the work. I know I'm not alone. I have found comfort in a maxim: *Almost everything will work again if you unplug it for a few minutes.* And of course that includes us.

Using technology to do virtual consulting deserves a book in itself. Some degree of working virtually is here to stay, including problems and benefits. Successful consultants in the future must mitigate the problems and capitalize on the benefits. To do so, they must be principled in character, competent in content, and skilled in delivery.

Regarding delivery, the challenge of virtual consulting is compounded by: 1. 24/7 connectivity that transcends time zones and location, so the consultant must always be *on*; 2. Technology can be complicated, unreliable, and difficult to use, so the quality of work performed may be reduced; 3. Bureaucracy and legal requirements can be so complex, confusing, and time-consuming that the consultant-client relationship suffers. Either the client or the consultant may conclude that the hassles are too great to achieve positive results; 4. Human relationships are often short and shallow, versus long and deep. Trust is the glue of effective interpersonal and group performance, requiring sufficient time and positive interactions to develop.

The technical challenges of virtual consulting are formidable, especially for international consultants and low-tech practitioners. So far, I'm OK, but just OK. Trying to keep up keeps my brain cells engaged and on red alert.

Do consultants learn from consultants? For sure, especially as they read each other's research, articles, and books, and as they compare notes — What are you doing about this? What did you do about that? What works well for you? Two examples make this point. I met Alan Zimmerman forty years ago at an IBM conference when he was conducting a seminar on communication and teamwork that was tailored for IBM managers. It was simply outstanding. Alan is a master of timeless principles for right living and working. I met Tom Morris the same year at a YPO International conference. Tom was a popular philosophy professor at Notre Dame with the ability to teach what philosophers across the ages would say about the issues and challenges of society today. Tom is wise and good in equal measure. Tom and Alan have successful consulting careers for three reasons: 1. They are self-transcendent men built for others; they are unselfish. 2. They have tremendous self-drive, self-discipline, and vitality; they work hard and stay current. 3. John Milton wrote in *Paradise Lost* — *The mind is its own place, and in itself can make a heaven of hell, a hell of heaven;* both Alan and Tom are heaven-makers.

#31

Evaluation Criteria for Consulting Services

From 1890 through the 1960s, the Cincinnati Milling Machine Company was one of the biggest producers of machine tools in the world. The company was renamed Cincinnati Milacron in 1970. I had the honor of working with the company in the areas of management development and employee training from 1976 to 1998. Cincinnati Milacron was known for excellence in employee and customer training, especially under the leadership of Jack Cahall, George Sederberg, Mike Ramundo, Al Aerni, and Paul Quealy.

In 1978, I used four criteria to evaluate the effectiveness of customer relations training – **Pace, Relevance, Value, and Participation.** I have used these criteria to plan, execute, and evaluate every consulting service I have provided since that time. **Pace** – activities must be paced just right – not too slow or too fast in the mind of the client. **Relevance** – the service provided must be considered important by the client, not a one-off or just a nice to do initiative. **Value** – clients judge service based on value, so are the results worth the time and money spent? **Participation** – clients must be intellectually, physically, and emotionally involved for maximum success; personal participation results in buy-in and follow-through.

I go over these four criteria with the client before beginning a service to be sure we are on the same wavelength. At the completion of the service, the client evaluates the pace, relevance, value, and participation on a 1 - 10 scale. The results are discussed – what to keep, what to drop, and what to change in the future. I enter this evaluation as well as project notes in the client's file. Notes include who did what, when, where, how, and why, as well as the fee. **Lesson learned: Clients appreciate a simple and logical approach to planning, executing, and evaluating consulting services. They think it's professional and gives them peace of mind to be guided by pace, relevance, value, and participation.**

#32

Joe Ward, Jimmy Stewart, and the Toyota News Story – The Power of the Pen

In 1996, I gave a talk at Toyota on the role of leadership in creating a high morale/ high-performance work culture. The title was *Building Community in the Workplace.* It featured the work of John Gardner, including the conditions necessary to create community: shared vision, wholeness incorporating diversity, shared culture, internal communications, consideration and trust, maintenance and government, participation and shared leadership, development of younger members, affirmations, and links with outside groups. People hunger for community and are more productive when they find it.

Joe Ward was a well-known *Louisville Courier-Journal* reporter who looked like Jimmy Stewart in a fedora hat and trench coat. Joe was distinctive using a pencil and pad to write his stories. His feature story on *Building Community* helped readers understand the importance of culture on work morale and job performance with special attention to the role of leadership. A variety of articles and news stories like this helped grow my consulting practice over the years.

In 1973, the Transportation Authority of Northern Kentucky (TANK) received a demonstration grant to promote public transportation. It was jointly sponsored by management and labor and was a success at building teamwork between operations and maintenance, as well as management and labor leaders. The intervention was a combination of human relations training and behavior modification. It included agreement on positive driver behaviors, self-reporting performance, and recognition for participation.

General Manager John Williams, Operations Manager Ray Lawrence, and Union President Jim Cummings worked together to achieve improvement in three areas: Passenger relations, employee teamwork, and a national record for increased ridership. Al Shottelkotte's WCPO News featured the story as a top 10 for the year, because driver interviews were human interest favorites. The TANK project was a model for similar passenger relations and employee teamwork training conducted from Washington D.C. to California, largely because of word-of-mouth support.

Lesson: There is a saying – *early to bed, early to rise, work hard and advertise.* **The best advertisement is word of mouth testimony and a good story**. Aesop, The Bible, Walt Disney, and the publishers of Children's Golden Books know the power of a memorable story.

#33

The 4th Most Important Year of my Life, 2000 – The Stern and Craggy Shores of Maine

The fourth most important year of my life was 2000, when our family moved to Maine. It was a grand adventure! We are Midwest folks, but the stern and craggy shores of Maine are stunningly beautiful and speak to us. Here's the story: Beginning in 1967, our family lived one year in a rented house next to a historic Cincinnati cemetery, thirteen years in a charming home on Mary Lane in the Village of Wyoming, eight years in a country home with a barn in Loveland, seven years on a rolling farm on Shady Lane in Kentucky, and five years on a large farm in Owen County. I wasn't raised on a farm, but Nancy always loved the country. As for me, every time I walked toward the John Deere tractor, someone thought of a better idea. Often, it was me.

When I came home from work one day in 1999, Nancy wondered what might be next. I was teaching and consulting heavily and retirement wasn't in the picture. She was thinking more north than south, and I thought Lake Geneva, Wisconsin might be a good fit – someday. My friend Dan Gregorie said the coast of Maine is glorious and we should take a trip there. My Son Larry and I visited the Mid-Coast and Downeast Maine in June and loved everything about the Acadia National Park area. I thought Nancy and I should visit in the winter Christmas break to test the climate. On average, Acadia National Park gets 100 inches of snow each year, the temperature average is 10 degrees colder than Cincinnati, and summer is a month shorter in Maine.

Nancy finked out on me and sent me. I didn't expect to buy a home, but the time to do it in Maine is when everything is under two feet of snow. A classic 1800 - 1830 New England cottage on the ocean was for sale and I bought it. When school was out in May, we sold both farms in Kentucky and moved to Maine. On the way there, we bought a painting with two bears dancing in the woods. We thought Friedrich Nietzsche was thinking about us when he wrote: *Those who were seen dancing were thought to be insane by those who could not hear the music.*

Maine worked out because two of our children, Larry and Heather, moved with us and our granddaughter Jessie was raised on the enchanting coast of Maine; our oldest son Page and grandson Bill visit each summer. It worked out also because there were three direct flights daily between Bangor and Cincinnati. I could take a 5:30 am flight, make a 9:00 am class at the university, and return to Maine at the end of the day. Nancy stayed in Maine full-time. I was a weekend Dad, but we saw it as a small price to pay for a little bit of heaven. Finally, the move to Maine worked out because I could continue teaching at the university and conduct my consulting practice from our ocean home. 2000 was an exciting year for our family, and it changed our lives permanently. We came to live and work in Maine, where we will always be.

Soon after moving to Maine, I had a sabbatical and worked from home. It was a glorious year, and I learned a human relations principle – **you don't have to attend every argument you are invited to.** Beginning in 2000, I have used the same New Year's resolution every year: **make war on my vices, keep peace in the family, and do good work with dear friends.** This works great!

#34

Using Outdoor Initiatives as a Personal Growth/OD (Organizational Development) Tool – Limits, Liabilities, and Testimonials

In 1976, I sponsored an Outward Bound course for Steve McMillen. It was an independent study using Outward Bound as a venue for personal growth. The location was the Rocky Mountains, and the themes were motivation, teamwork, leadership, and integrity. Steve's report supported the value of Outward Bound as a 'growth through challenge' experience based on the motto, "To serve, to strive, and not to yield." Gordon Barnhart is a master of using outdoor challenge as an organizational development tool, drawing on his experiences working with street gangs, serving as a Captain in the U.S. Special Forces, and being grounded deeply in his understanding of people. His insights have been a great help to me.

North Carolina State University – In 1988, I was asked by Charles Leffler to facilitate a team-building and visioning retreat for the NC State Finance and Administration executive leaders. Day One was a morning 'low course' challenging the group to work effectively as a team. The afternoon was a 'high course' in the trees, challenging personal ability and courage. Day one closed with a short debrief and observations about the morning and afternoon experiences.

Day two was devoted to the creation of a Finance and Administration vision and strategy to succeed document. This was to include agreement on direction, critical success factors, and elements of a supportive work culture. I didn't expect the scene at breakfast: 40-year-olds were praising the previous day's teamwork, 50-year-olds were recounting how they overcame fear, and 60-year-olds were bragging about their climbing styles – did you see the way I hung on that limb!?

It was evident that the previous day had been a memorable experience for everyone – and they were in the mood to work together to create a positive, future-focused vision and take practical steps to be successful. **My conclusion was: Are outdoor challenges and growth experiences safe? Semi. Are they for every team and individual member? No. Are they effective team-building experiences? Generally. Was it good for the people I observed? Yes.**

Ten Broeck – A similar teambuilding exercise was conducted for the staff of Ten Broeck Hospital in Louisville, Kentucky, 2003 (Ten Broeck is the name of a famous thoroughbred racehorse). It didn't include 'high course' challenges, but the 'low course' challenges were appropriately demanding. Creative obstacles required communication, teamwork, and a one-team attitude that helped on the job challenges back at work. It was a successful day of goodwill and learning. Then came a surprise: The day was hot and I had worn a white t-shirt and blue sweatshirt. The combination of sweat and blue dye from the sweatshirt made my arms blue. I couldn't figure out why and imagined all sorts of troubling causes. Several showers and lots of soap fixed my arms, to my great relief. **I learned that when unexpected things happen, don't panic. Think about cause and effect and study the situation. When I**

looked at my arms and then at the wet sweatshirt, I made the dye connection ... thank goodness.

Trust Walk – The Kentucky Horse Park after hours is an ideal place to conduct a 'trust walk' team-building exercise. It has interesting structures, textures, smells, and sounds to create an obstacle course through which sighted partners lead blind-folded partners only by voice. Pairs of participants build trust by helping each other. In 2002, Bluegrass Area Development Director Jas Sekhon and I conducted a team-building exercise followed by a group discussion to reinforce positive relationships between staff members to better serve the planning and technical assistance needs of the Bluegrass region of Kentucky. It was a grand success with an important lesson: **Outdoor learning initiatives must be safe above all. With guided discussion, they can help build positive relationships and effective teamwork in the workplace.**

Van Melle – In 1997, this one surprised me, because I had no idea it was coming, although I should have because Van Melle was that happy company from Holland that made great candy. Marius Van Melle was the second son of the owner of Holland's largest candy maker, a lot like Hershey and Mars in the U.S., and was in charge of North American operations. Marius was loved by his employees and was a great motivator. Participative leadership came naturally to him, so he scheduled an afternoon, evening, and full-day management retreat focused on teamwork, goal setting, and accountability. Shortly after dinner, and during a deep discussion about customers and products, everyone jumped up at once, looked at each other, and ran for their hidden weapons – giant water guns. In the war in the woods that followed, whoever was the driest after 20 minutes won the prize – tickets to a Cincinnati Reds baseball game. Adults became like teenagers squirting each other in glee. A whistle was blown after 20 minutes, and the group reconvened. An intense and highly effective discussion followed that helped guide the company to achieve record performance. **The lesson learned is the value of fun – the war in the woods released tension, helped the group laugh, and increased camaraderie. When they returned to business, they were more spontaneous, interactive, and productive.**

Cianbro – The following is an example of field learning that I will always remember. I don't know where to begin with the feelings I had about the Civil War battle at Gettysburg – humility, gratitude, respect, sadness, and, most keenly, reverence. Leadership talks on such subjects as purpose, strategy, communication, resilience, conviction, and courage went well and the discussion was deep. High points were bonding as the group walked the battlefield together, learning history from the Park Service guides, especially at the National Cemetery where Abraham Lincoln delivered the Gettysburg Address, and staying at a farmhouse where everyone could talk a ton and apply what was learned to advance the company. The retreat was facilitated by Mark Brooks, a military scholar, expert on the battle of Gettysburg, and superb educator. Senior executives Mike Bennett, Andi Vigue, and Pete Vigue sponsored the retreat so emerging leaders could learn and grow together to best serve the company with honor, responsibility, and leadership effectiveness. All but one of us had never been to Gettysburg and we felt blessed for the experience.

#35

Consulting for Trade – Barbecue Ribs, Hotel Hospitality, and Dental Care

Consulting for trade is not uncommon, especially with retail and service organizations. Three examples are:

1. Barbeque Ribs

My first consulting for trade was with Montgomery Inn, a unique and popular restaurant in Cincinnati, founded in 1951. The great success of the restaurant is traced to the warm personality and secret barbecue sauce of the Mother Matula, the colorful and outgoing personality of the Father Ted, and the hard work of two great sons, Tom and Dean, who grew up in the business from dishwashing to management to ownership. The Montgomery Inn is enormously successful as a destination restaurant that sells more barbecue sauce than Heinz sells ketchup in the Cincinnati/Northern Kentucky area. Sports heroes like Oscar Robertson and the Big Red Machine, Hollywood legends like Bob Hope and Frank Sinatra, political figures like Ronald Reagan and George Bush, astronauts like Neil Armstrong and John Glenn, and hundreds of loyal families wait in line for Montgomery Inn ribs (or order these to be sent to the White House). Tom and Dean Gregory thought a Saturday seminar would be good to reinforce communication and teamwork for all staff members. In exchange, I received barbecue ribs. For a year, I would take home barbecue sandwiches (our favorites) for the family. A year later, we did this again – Saturday training for barbecue ribs. Montgomery Inn is famous for a reason . . . you can't get enough of their barbecue sauce, loin back ribs, and hospitality.

2. Hotel Hospitality

When our family moved from Grant County to Owen County, the distance to Northern Kentucky University was farther than I could manage every day. I could handle a full schedule of morning classes, evening commitments, and an hour commute each way, but an hour and a half commute each way was too much. When I told Nancy, her response was that I should think how much fun it would be when I got home. Thank goodness, Choice Hotels offered me a place to stay when I needed it, in exchange for staff development and leadership training. This arrangement was a godsend for five years. When we moved to Maine, it was continued with the Radisson Brand. Again, thank goodness for good hospitality and comfort for the weary consultant!

3. Dental Care

In 2010, I needed three dental implants. This was an expensive proposition, but Northern Kentucky Oral and Maxillofacial Surgery Associates offered to provide these in exchange for a seminar/workshop on The Human Side of Dental Care. The participants were the Dentists and Staff members of the Dental offices in Northern Kentucky. A Saturday retreat was held at the Summit

Hills Country Club with the title 'Our Summit Awaits'. The themes were communication, teamwork, and patient care. Sub-themes were: 1. Honesty- share the truth; 2. Perspective- know the difference between passion and obsession; 3. Trust- what matters are the promises we keep, not the promises we make; 4. Focus- manage fear by focusing on what is important; and 5. Humility- appreciate the people who help you succeed. The day was participative, enjoyable, and highly helpful in coordinating dental care in Northern Kentucky. I was thankful for the opportunity to provide consulting service in exchange for the highest possible dental care.

Lesson learned: Funding for consulting services can be creative, including consulting for trade and third party payment. Two examples of third party payment from aviation are: 1. The consulting fee for an American Airlines Association Executive conference in Minnesota was paid by the company providing signage for airports across the nation; and 2. The consulting fee for an Airport Owners International conference in Seattle was paid by AT&T, who provided public phones in all U.S. airports at the time. Both organizations were warmly recognized for sponsoring education for the aviation industry.

An important note: IRS requires reporting services for trade.

#36

Attention and Effort – Work to Learn/Work to Remember

From about 1967 to about 1987 (20 years), I worked diligently to learn what to do and how to do it as a consultant. To prepare for clients, I studied materials and methods for days including intensely the night before, to execute well. From about 2002 to about 2022 (20 years), I worked equally hard to remember what to do and how to do it. I reviewed materials and methods thoroughly including the night before to execute well.

There was a period of time in the intervening years from about 1987 to 2002 (15 years) when I didn't have to work as hard to either learn or remember materials and methods; preparation was easy as my learning was high, and my memory was good. Those days are gone, and I am definitely in the work hard to review and work hard to remember category at this stage in my life.

What about today? I find 'memory' to be a mixed blessing: I must concentrate fully and with purpose and use post-it notes galore, but I have experienced so much in the past that what I remember is often the perfect solution to today's challenge. **The lesson is there is a short period in your career when preparation** is easy, but most of the time you will be working hard to learn, or you will be working equally hard to remember so that your work is always well done.

#37

SERDI (SouthEast Regional Director's Institute) Lifelong Learning – 9/11, Government Accounting 101, and Virginia's Black Box

I enjoy learning new things and sharing these with others. From government client SERDI – SouthEast Regional Director's Institute, I've learned about a variety of subjects: 1. 9/11 details; 2. Quirks in government accounting; 3. Virginia Tech's virtual reality black box; 4. Cuban cigars in Miami; 5. Kentucky thoroughbred auctions; 6. Beach volleyball in Hilton Head; 7. Historic Williamsburg; 8. Georgia peaches; and 9. Kentucky bourbon. Mahatma Gandhi gives good advice: **Learn as if you were going to live forever . . . live as if you were going to die tomorrow. A core characteristic of every successful consultant I've known is the love of learning. If you don't love to learn and keep on learning, don't become a consultant. It's not good for you or the client.**

Closely related to learning is personal development. Leo Tolstoy observed that everybody thinks about changing humanity, but nobody thinks about changing himself. The consultant can help by viewing life as a novel being written in the ink of the moment, and serving as a positive role model for life-long personal and professional growth.

#38

Dodging Stones – Courts, Corrections, and CitiCorp

I've had two run-ins with kidney stones. In 1974, I completed a training day for King Kwik store managers. It was a glorious day, and I had no clue what was going to happen next. After everyone left, I was washing my hands in the washroom when I felt a pain like a mule kick in my lower abdomen. I was young and had never heard of kidney stones. I was doubled over in pain when Sam Vinci checked on me. The ambulance ride to the hospital was a torture trip as we seemed to hit every road bump and hole in Cincinnati. All was well when the stones passed the next morning.

The second attack occurred 30 years later on a Sunday. The pain was familiar, so I drove to the hospital emergency room. I was placed on a table in a waiting room. No pain relief could be provided till the kidney stones could be seen in X-rays. This took a long time because the emergency room was full. The pain was so great that I remember thinking, "I've had a good life." I was released with instructions to check for stones after every bathroom trip. It was summer and I had three clients to serve the following three days – Citicorp, Kentucky Corrections, and the Clermont County Court.

Two lessons were learned: 1. Medical emergencies can happen to anyone, at any time, and any place; 2. If medical problems can be worked around, do so. If it's humanly possible to meet client needs, the consultant must deliver. This is appreciated and the reward is mutual loyalty. My first consulting assignment with the Urology Group was in 1992 when we had a staff retreat focused on patient care and working together effectively. Everyone still remembers the skits the staff prepared to show professionalism, teamwork, and clinical excellence. Working with Bill Monnig, Ed Elicker, Joe Creevy, and Earl Walz for over thirty years has been an honor beyond words to describe.

#39

Stretched in Nashville – The Night it Couldn't Be Done

As a consultant, I've been guided by the words of St. Francis of Assisi: Start by doing what is necessary; then do what is possible; suddenly you will be doing the impossible. However, there was one time I thought I might not make a consulting or teaching commitment. Tony Noel of McGraw-Hill, publisher of *The Art of Leadership*, asked me to work with Savant Learning Systems to provide video tutorials to support the text. These would be used by instructors to complement the text, including for online courses. McGraw-Hill thought Nassar Nassar's company had created the best pedagogy to deliver college and university courses, combining the course text, author tutorials, and assigned course instructors.

The format was the author of the text (accounting, biology, economics, etc.) would provide an introductory lecture to the book and create fifteen 30 - 40-minute televised talks based on the content. Graphics and embedded links to supporting materials were added by Savant Learning designers. Instructors could use the text and tutorials as the backbone of their courses and add complementary materials as appropriate. The television studio was top-grade, and the media production staff was outstanding. The problem was that I didn't know I would be asked to provide the introductory lecture in the studio the next morning and film 15 video tutorials the following three days. I didn't have an introductory lecture written, typed, and ready to read from the teleprompter when I returned from dinner and started on the script at 9:00 pm.

The hotel was a popular place with Nashville celebrities, including Garth Brooks on site, but I resisted distraction. The introductory lecture was critical, and it had to be right. I was still working on it at 5:00 am. I called Nancy at 3:00 am for moral support and it helped immensely. I finished the script at 7:00 am and gave it to Savant Learning professionals to type into the teleprompter. I have enormous admiration and gratitude for the talent, teamwork, and dedication of the Savant Learning System staff. They were 'the best' at what they did. **The lesson I learned was that fatigue is real – the inability to do more work because of previous work. From 2:00 am to 3:00 am, my thoughts were blurry, and I could barely keep my eyes open. I was seriously worried about my ability to deliver on a commitment. One must be rested to work well.**

#40

Be a Learner – The Importance of Books

After basic biology, the three determinants of a human life are 1. *What we tell ourselves that we believe.* Some people talk themselves into diminished lives, saying you're too this and not enough that, to the point of depression; others recognize their deficiencies, but focus on their assets, saying you've got your problems, but in the main you're OK . . . and look at those strengths! 2. *The people we are around.* Some people will tear us down if given a chance; others will make our lives great. There's much truth in the saying that we become the average of our five best friends, so we should surround ourselves with positive and caring people and be that way for others. 3. *The books we read (and by extension, other forms of media).* Garbage in and garbage out. Some books and media are greatly helpful and enhance our lives with knowledge and skills; others are harmful with poisonous content and false information. Knowing the importance of these three determinants has helped me to help others in their professional and personal development. **Lesson: Positive self-talk, family and friends, and good books help us live full and meaningful lives.**

One day, not too long ago, a favorite student from my early years as a professor asked me to make a list of the books that have shaped me. I thought it was a strange request, but I said yes. When I gave Earl Walz the list, he said he wanted to share it with his children. It was an enormous compliment and I enjoyed making the list, which was a form of a library, a curated selection of great books to be shared with others. Earl had kept in touch, to my great satisfaction. And that allowed me to influence another generation of his family. A practice I recommend for everyone is to keep in touch with your mentors.

Bertrand Russell is famous for saying the good life is inspired by love and guided by knowledge. Books that have influenced me as a consultant are history, philosophy, psychology, and business books. I have used all of the books in Appendix A in some meaningful way as a consultant on the human side of work. Some were used early in my career, others later. I can remember the context and usefulness of each book as an aid in helping others. **Lesson: There is a saying that a book read at the right time can change everything that follows. Ideas, truths, principles, metaphors, and exercises in books can be tailored to the needs and circumstances of the client. Every successful consultant has a similar library.**

As a Labor representative at Ford Motor Company from 1966 to 1969, I enjoyed sharing books with UAW union representatives. We talked about *The Naked Ape*, *The Art of Loving*, *The Little Prince*, and other books as they related to the world of work. It was fun to watch them hide the books in their shirts when they left my office, not wanting their members to know they were reading Henrik Ibsen's *A Doll's House*, Anne Morrow Lindbergh's *Gift from the Sea*, and Viktor Frankl's *Man's Search for Meaning*. When I left Ford in 1969, UAW International Representative Harry Hacke said we were ten years ahead of our time. UAW Plant Chairman Gil Sizemore said discussing the ideas and information in good books helped create goodwill, satisfying relationships, and a more productive workplace. I learned a lot in these discussions that helped me later as a consultant on the human side of work. **Lesson Learned: Everyone needs a library, especially a consultant.**

There are two kinds of books – one for the hour and one for life. For me, *Man's Search for Meaning* has been a book for life. In 1963, Viktor Frankl reminded our class: Everything you do goes down in history, and, in that sense, is irretrievable. This was a profound thought that registered deeply. Since then, my goal has been to live an examined and meaningful life, neither error free nor one of regrets, proving the power of books to change all that follows.

A sample book story – I was discussing the lessons in *The One Minute Manager* by Ken Blanchard with the management team of Bank One in the Greater Cincinnati area in 1983. When the president of the bank arrived late, he sat in the back of the room while I explained the four factors of the one-minute reprimand. Suddenly, he jumped to his feet and said, "That book works! Everyone here knows I'm late because I was in Columbus with the Chairman of the Company. I was being corrected, an experience that usually isn't pleasant. All the way from Columbus to Cincinnati, I thought about constructive steps I could take to improve, and I wasn't upset. As George was talking, I remembered seeing *The One Minute Manager* on the Chairman's desk. This book works for leaders in all Bank functions and all levels of responsibility." That was an instant boost for my teaching. The consulting project was management development, team building, and improving bank performance.

The *Hard Hat* by Jon Gordon is a superb book for use in leadership development and team building, including senior executive teams. Individuals in highly visible and influential groups must be role models for working together effectively and excellent leadership behavior. Their organizations are watching and are impacted greatly by what they see. The *Hard Hat* is inspirational, educational, and tremendously useful for organizational development.

#41

Every Consultant's Dilemma – How Much to Charge

In 1970, I faced a dilemma all consultants have – how much to charge. I answered this by asking myself how much I would be happy to pay. I didn't want to overcharge because I didn't want the client to be focused on the cost versus the work being done. I didn't want to undercharge because I had a family to raise and time and effort were finite. As a professor, I had one day a week in the Fall and Spring, and three days a week in the Summer that could be devoted to consulting. The marketplace influences fees charged for consulting services. From the beginning, I've charged a daily fee that has included preparation time, unless extensive work is required such as psychological assessments, interviews, and focus groups. I've raised this amount four times over 52 years. I view myself much like a journeyman with journeyman fees, never as a celebrity whose fees are much higher. I've been able to keep my fees low because I have few expenses as a professor.

There are four ways consultants are usually paid: 1. Billable hours; 2. Type of intervention; 3. Retainer based on a period of service; 4. Percentage of financial gain (in the private sector). Most consultants charge and are paid based on billable hours. Accountants, engineers, and lawyers are examples. Many other consultants are paid based on the delivery of a service or product. Speakers and writers are examples. A few consultants are paid based on the percentage of financial improvement gained from their work by the client. Examples are business and investment consultants. Some consultants are hired to fulfill functional duties on a temporary basis such as one day per week, two weeks per month, and 1 to 12 months per year. Examples range from nurses to executives.

From the beginning, I have used the second approach – an honorarium plus expenses. I would never charge more than I would be willing to pay. If someone assisted or partnered in the effort, the client would pay the same total amount, and this would be divided by the providers, based on contribution. Change in schedule and cancellation fees are important subjects for clients and consultants, recognizing that unexpected and unavoidable events happen – weather, sickness, accidents, etc. There is typically no fee when rescheduling is required. A reasonable guideline for cancellation is: No fee when cancellation notice is provided before one month; half-fee if cancellation notice is provided less than one month, unless the event is rescheduled for full fee.

What about virtual meeting cancellations? Virtual presentations, interviews, and coaching have become commonplace in today's environment. Cancellation disrupts schedules and equates to loss of time and opportunity. Consultant Rob Followell provides practical guidance: No penalties for clients rescheduling with at least 24-hour notice. For clients rescheduling with less than 24-hour notice, reschedule without penalty if there is no pattern of cancellations.

I have followed three practices regarding money: 1. Keep costs as low as reasonably possible, because what matters is not the top line billed, but the profits after costs. 2. Keep client reimbursed expenses as low as possible and provide meticulous receipts. This practice was tremendously helpful when I was audited by IRS on two different occasions. Both audits were painless because I kept good records. Record keeping isn't a natural strength for me, but It's important to do. 3. There are times when my fee is too high for a client. I have three responses: a. Refer the client to another qualified consultant, b. Provide the service for a reduced amount that is given by the client as a scholarship or grant to a worthy person or cause, c. Provide the service at no cost. I only do this when an organization has no funds and serious needs (such as the free store or a homeless shelter).

There were two times in fifty-two years that a client failed to pay what was owed. In both cases, the individuals who hired me moved to different government agencies and replacement personnel failed to pay the bills, although the amounts were undisputed and new administrators were apologetic. When the bills were still not paid after a year, I wrote both bills off as business losses. The amounts were small, thank goodness. **What did I learn? The client who hires you may not be present to pay you, and neither an agreement letter nor a signed contract is a guarantee of payment. If it's a molehill, don't make it a mountain – let it go.**

I've been guided by this thought since 1970: **Do what you love (learn and teach), for the right reasons (morale and productivity), in the right way (others' interests first), and *enough* money will follow. So, how much should you charge? No more than you would be willing to pay.**

A postscript about money – when I arrived early at an IBM Management Conference held at Smith College in 1982, Fred Young was addressing the audience. He looked like the Chicago banker he was (Director of the Trust Department of the Harris National Bank) and he spoke with the wit and dry humor of Mark Twain. You couldn't *not* listen to Fred. Everyone was riveted to every word and was taking notes. Within minutes, I was as well.

Fred said he would rather be old and rich than old and poor.

If we agreed, we should pay attention. He said that as Chief Trust Officer of the bank, he had observed three ways of getting rich: 1. Inherit wealth; 2. Marry wealth; and 3. Earn wealth. The three most common ways of earning wealth are to build a successful business, own and develop real estate, and invest money intelligently. Fred went on to say that it's just as important to wisely manage the money you have as it is to earn it. He said it's not what you make that counts; it's the difference between what you make and how you spend it that will do great things for you.

Fred's formula for financial management is simple and doable: 1. First, invest at least 15 percent of every dollar you receive in interest and dividend-providing vehicles; 2. Next, spend income received on absolutely necessary purchases, such as health, food, housing, and transportation; 3. Next, spend income received on developmental activities, such as education, including your children; 4. Next, spend income received on reasonable discretionary purchases such as clothes, cars, hobbies, and travel; 5. Remaining money should be used to build wealth and be available for emergencies; 6. If you must borrow, do so wisely and never buy on credit that has interest charges. The key is to invest first, then spend income within your means.

Fred thought happiness begins with feeling good about oneself, and fundamental to this is practicing good financial management. It helps to invest and spend wisely as soon as possible, even though there are examples of well-known people who gain wealth later in life (Fred cited Colonel Sanders of Kentucky Fried Chicken). In contrast, most rich people postpone gratification early in life to gain financial security later in life. By being wise and responsible, people can have healthy and happy families.

I'm thankful that Fred befriended me and that I followed his financial advice thereafter. Fred died at age 98, surrounded by family and dear friends. He would want me to pass this guidance onward – work, earn, invest, enjoy! **Financial peace of mind is important to a consultant because the needs of the client must be the number 1 focus of concern and effort, not personal money matters.**

#42

Records Count – Keep Them!

The palest ink is more powerful than the best memory. Clients will forget things over time, and will appreciate it immensely when you have records – what was the issue, what action steps were taken, who was involved, what were the results? What were the costs? I've kept records on every consulting assignment since 1970. A one-page summary answering who did what, when, where, how, and why is a tremendous job aid for the consultant and client. **Lesson: I don't know a successful consultant who doesn't keep good records.**

My friend and long-time accountant Cliff Stone developed Alzheimer's disease over our last three years together. We didn't know why we were inefficient and so forgetful those years, but I learned the importance of keeping good personal records and copies of all financial documents, and still do. Good judgment can come from experience and a lot of that comes from bad judgment. Good judgment is to save time, solve problems, and build goodwill by keeping good records.

#43

Consultant-Client Compact

Consulting services are usually based on a contract; often it's unwritten – a mental or physical handshake. It's best if it's in writing, if only confirmed by an email or letter. In any case, there is a compact that agreed-upon services will be provided for an agreed-upon payment. A good compact requires an unambiguous alignment of consulting services with client needs. It's astounding how much consulting is done that is wasteful and even contrary to the client's best interests. To prevent this, two questions must be answered: Does the consultant fully understand the vision, mission, values, goals, critical success factors, and culture of the client? Do the consultant's efforts support these elements in a meaningful way for a reasonable fee? If the answer to these two questions is yes, make a client-consultant compact and go forward. If not, save time, money, and dissatisfaction – stop.

Organizational consulting focuses on quality of work and quality of work life issues. This often involves personal, interpersonal, and organizational development and may include coaching. It's important to have agreement on roles, goals, and practical guidelines for the client and consultant relationship. Who is the client? The client is the entity paying for the service (usually the organization). The subject(s) are the focus and beneficiaries of the service (usually employees of the organization). The consultant is the provider of service (guided by the principle, never do harm). Because mutual trust is important, confidentiality is maintained, except to prevent harm. Organizational consulting doesn't include psychotherapy or legal advice, as these are properly referred to mental health and legal service professionals.

It's important for an organization to have a policy that provides clear and practical guidance for the use of consultants. This includes who can hire consultants, and the do's and don'ts for engaging and monitoring services. The bigger or more dispersed an organization is, the more important this is to avoid confusion, consulting creep (hiring more consulting service than is necessary), and communication problems, as the following case shows.

The senior management of a large public utility launched a company-wide initiative with two goals: Improve employee morale and improve company performance. There are many methods that can be used to do this including job enrichment, management by objectives, total quality management, gainsharing, employee engagement, lean operation, performance management, coaching, balanced scorecard, appreciative inquiry, six sigma quality, project management, action research, checklist procedures, and behavior modification. All of these techniques are effective when they are understood, owned, worked on, and supported at every level of the leadership pyramid – top executives, middle managers, and frontline supervisors. This company chose participative management and team building as its means to improve.

Fifteen cross-functional groups of employees at all levels of responsibility were formed and charged to identify a significant problem (bottleneck or practice) that was reducing employee morale or company performance. They were provided the time and resources to determine the causes of the problem – manpower (people), methods (procedures), materials (supplies), equipment (machines), recommend solution(s), take agreed-upon action, monitor progress, and report results. The groups were charged to use participative management and teamwork techniques. Ample time, resources, and senior management attention were allocated to this two-year initiative involving all levels of personnel from all walks of the company. Each group was assigned a professional consultant who was charged to facilitate the work and learning of the group.

No two consultants came from the same firm or background and the different styles, tools, and processes they used were sometimes counter-productive to the company. They were all singing from the same hymnal with purpose and conviction and great talent, but they were on different pages. I was one of those ineffective consultants. After much confusion and waste of resources, the company addressed the problem so that fifteen consultants would fly in formation and in the right direction. It took direct company intervention with regularly scheduled and well-run communication sessions to manage the services of their fifteen qualified but independent consultants. The initiative was a great success, but it almost failed because the company didn't effectively coordinate the services of the independent consultants during the first six months of the initiative.

Lesson learned: A company must manage its consultants, or consultants will manage the company. Consultants may be expert and well-meaning, but clients must stay intentionally involved to manage their services for the best results. A clearly understood client-consultant compact is indispensable. Since doing this project in 1992, I have communicated proactively with other consultants serving an organization in the same area, making sure our efforts are aligned and mutually supportive for the client's benefit.

#44

The Fit Consultant

Like many young married men, I started picking up weight from 1967 to 1980. I changed my waist size twice. In addition, my blood pressure was high. At about that time, I began writing the book *Stress without Distress: Rx for Burnout*. I decided to get back in shape, myself. As part of the book, I added a **1 x 3 x 7 = 21** plan for dealing with stress. I saw too many people spending the first half of their lives building their wealth and losing their health, only to spend the second half of their lives losing their wealth to regain their health. Too many people who should know better eat too much, sleep too little, neglect their bodies, and fall into negative and self-defeating behaviors.

I resolved to follow the plan personally:

1) at least once a day, use positive imagery to count my blessings;

x 3) at least three times a week, do physical exercise, including aerobic exercise for cardiovascular health;

x 7) have the equivalent of seven restful nights of sleep each week (this is still a challenge);

= 21) have the equivalent of twenty-one nutritious meals per week. This regimen improved my health when I was 37 and has helped me maintain the physical fitness required to be a healthy parent, professor, and consultant. No matter where I am – at home or on the road – I follow this plan.

Beginning in 1977, I added an additional habit for mental and spiritual fitness. At every consulting engagement, I walk the beach, woods, or park to clear my mind and interact with nature. This is a great way to maintain balance and perspective. Walking beaches from Bermuda to Hawaii, and hiking trails from California to Maine, help keep me physically and mentally fit. I will remember forever walking the grounds of the Battle of Vicksburg, the streets of the village of Williamsburg, the beaches of St. John and Puerto Rico, the trails of the Black Forest, and the monuments of Washington D.C. These and so many other walks and runs help me maintain mental and physical fitness.

A word about safety: An evening run in Louisville in 1978 proved to be a problem when I tripped and scraped my right arm. The flight to Virginia the next day went well, but by the following morning, my arm was blue and nearly twice its normal size. I couldn't wear a white shirt because the pain was intense. We changed the two-day event to one, and I flew to a Cincinnati hospital that evening – proof that a consultant should be safety conscious and fit to work.

Physical safety is increasingly important, especially for consultants who travel. A fire at the Beverly Hills Supper Club in Southgate, Kentucky, May 28, 1977 (165 people died, 200 were injured) and a shooting rampage at IBM in Bethesda, Maryland, May 29,

1982 (killing 2, wounding 8) made me permanently conscious of physical safety. I had given a Kentucky Real Estate talk on leadership at the Beverly Hills Club several weeks before the fire; and I gave a management talk at IBM in Bethesda several weeks after the shooting spree. Regarding fire safety thereafter, I always check the exits before every meeting and before sleeping at night. Regarding violence safety, I've memorized the three-point priority response taught by law enforcement experts: first run, second hide, third fight with all your might.

Many consultants must travel. Some will say, "Sign me up!"; others will say, "No way, I need to sleep in my own bed every night." If travel is required, you must welcome adventure and be ready for anything. In my case, increasing age and increasing technology have combined to make travel an increasing challenge. No two showers and alarm clocks are the same, cell phones and GPS are boons, but headaches if you don't know how to use them. Roads in and out of cities and airports are like bowls of spaghetti to navigate with routes changing from week to week. Rental cars have become more reliable, but are more complicated to operate.

When you travel, you must plan well, but remain attentive, because surprises are common. When unexpected events happen (weather delays, schedule changes, human errors, etc.), you must stay calm, take things in stride, and not become over-stressed. Unnecessary alarm and constant vigilance can lead to exhaustion, including health problems and too rapid aging. This is why stress management and coping techniques are important for consultants to master.

A silver lining in travel is that mental challenges keep your brain cells popping. My 'go to' thought is always, "If this doesn't kill me, it will make me strong." This thought brings comfort when the road gets rough, as it often does. There is no question, you must be mentally fit to travel safely and traveling can help keep your brain stimulated and working well.

In 1995, Viktor Frankl was 90 years old. He was frustrated because he could no longer travel safely to give his talks and discussions about Logotherapy. Physical conditions precluded this and he was more than a little unhappy. Like many consultants and professors, Viktor Frankl loved to learn and teach, learn and teach, and this required travel he could no longer do. I relate to mobility with every passing year. I've never had trouble getting my mind on a task, and my heart seems to be immediately 'all in' when it comes to teaching and consulting. It's getting my body from point A to point B that is the increasing challenge. Weather, transportation, and physical limits can be formidable foes.

The following story is about health and leadership. In 1986, I felt queasy when I caught an early evening flight from Cincinnati to Delaware. By the time I arrived at the hotel that evening, I was thoroughly sick. I went to sleep praying for recovery by morning. When my client, Bob Taylor of the Delaware Department of Transportation, picked me up, I was gray and green and could barely function. The project focused on performance improvement of the transit system through effective leadership and employee teamwork. I was useless and Bob and his employees carried the day. Bob was a quiet and competent leader who taught caring leadership by his actions better than any textbook could. The employees responded with consideration and teamwork better than any lecture could teach. **I learned three lessons: When you're sick, you can't function. Out of adversity comes growth. Good people make good leaders and good employees, and together they make great companies.**

Two physical conditions that fall under fitness are dizziness and laryngitis. I mention these because each has happened to me twice and they are definite problems when the consultant must function well, such as when giving a speech or conducting a meeting. They are usually minor health problems, but I think about them every time I'm going to give a talk. My first case of laryngitis occurred in Boulder, Colorado at an IBM management conference in 1985. I went to dinner in the mountains the evening before and by the time I fell asleep, I had no voice. I woke up with almost no voice, but a microphone could amplify it enough to get the job done. There is an empathy gene in IBM leaders, and it worked out OK, but I learned to protect my vocal cords the days before a speech. I learned to rest my voice and drink lots of water. My first case of dizziness was when I was giving a talk to physician leaders at the University of Cincinnati in 2001. I didn't know the cause, but I thought 'I'm with the right audience.' In general, one should sit or lie down with eyes closed and drink lots of water. I sat down, drank lots of water and the dizziness disappeared. Thereafter, I drink lots of water before giving a talk and keep a full glass close. **Lessons learned: If you are addressing a group, protect your voice and drink lots of water.**

Beginning in 2012, I learned the importance of physical mobility. My right hip hurt so much that I struggled to make it from plane to plane in an airport. Lifting Nancy from bed to chair (we called it flying) resulted in the need for a hip replacement at Christ Hospital in Cincinnati in 2017. It was a grand success, thanks to Patrick Kirk and his operating team. Mobility was restored completely. Also, as I got older cataract removal was required. I went from a blurry world to seeing like a hawk, thanks to Larry Piazza and his eye care team. Modern medicine is miraculous, and it helps a lot if a consultant is mobile and sees well. **Lesson learned: good health is critical for successful consulting, and a key is to have a primary care physician who knows you well. Bob Wones was my physician for 35 years before retiring. He was a wise, caring, and 'less is more' Doctor who made sure I stayed healthy.**

Will Rogers puts being fit in perspective: If you don't think every day is a good one, try missing one. Not too long ago, I read the Tibetan secret to living long and well. It's good for consultants to know: Eat half, walk double, laugh triple, and love without measure.

#45

The Need for Mindfulness

When I was a young consultant, I learned the importance of focus and attention. It didn't come naturally, but I had so many details to keep track of as a parent, professor, and consultant that I needed to be mindful of what I was doing at all times and take notes. When I was in my middle years, the value of mindfulness and note-taking was reinforced due to a heavy work schedule and significant family health needs. As an older consultant, professor, and grandfather, mindfulness and note-taking are still in demand as experience has shown.

In 2021, I was walking on a path in the woods and was not being mindful when I tripped on a tree root. One minute I was perpendicular and the next I was flat on the ground. It made a good safety story the next day at a leadership class when I could remind the participants – children and grandparents need to watch where they walk and pick up their feet. **The lesson learned: Being mindful is not only a spiritual concept, but also a practical principle for safe behavior.**

Related to mindfulness is remembering things. One night in

1980, I woke up with a brilliant idea. In the morning, I couldn't remember it. **Lesson: Coincidentally with the introduction of post-it notes that year, I've kept a notepad and pencil with me at all times and places – bed stand, bathroom, kitchen, and car. You never know when you will have a thought or idea that must be captured.** Along these lines, there's something about the last fifteen minutes of a flight or a walk on the beach – good ideas become clear and present in remarkable detail. That's when I must write these thoughts on paper or lose them forever.

#46

Client Personalities

People sometimes ask: What are clients like? The answer is no two are the same. Every client and consultant has a unique interest, ruling passion, or is quirky in his or her own way. It makes them charming and is how we remember them. Clients think of my love of coffee, books, and family in reverse order. Some examples:

- Alan Burton of Cianbro loves scratch golf and an orderly workshop.
- Ron Seal of Texoma Medical loves root beer floats and LSU football.
- Jim Youngquist of SERDI loves Wildcat basketball and Lexington, Kentucky.
- Rick Woychik of the National Institutes of Health loves cars and science.
- Terri Bonar-Stewart of Transit loves her red truck and her sisters.
- Pete Vigue of Cianbro loves granite and will never say can't.
- Dick Boyle of AEP loves socks and his toolbelt.

- Jim Patton of vocational education loves careers for kids.
- Walt Lovenberg of Marion Merrell Dow loves science and exotic food.
- Dan Ronay of Indiana Corrections loves the Marines.
- Wayne Carlisle of Maxim Crane loves bulldozers and horses.
- Charlie Leffler of NC State loves Disney World and world travel.
- Jeff Walter of Great American Insurance loves fishing and swimming.
- Kerry Gillihan of Cardinal Hill loves turkey hunting and fly fishing.
- Gordy Snyder of Commonwealth Hotels loves his dog and boat.
- Pete Jordon of Choice Hotels loves his boat and the beach.
- Rob Followell of the Followell Group loves singing in the band and white-water rafting.
- Tom Black of Washington Metropolitan Transit loves trains and wine.
- Richard Jackson of Marion Merrell Dow loves science and the St. Louis Cardinals.
- Chuck Hewett of the Jackson Lab loves scuba diving and skiing.
- David Hosea of Hosea Worldwide loves impossible tasks and moving anything.
- Fred Gilliam of Austin loves buses and people.
- Alen Saric of Hyatt loves kids and books.
- Tim Holbrook of the Kentucky Legislative Research Commission loves golf and church.
- Florence Jones of Methodist Health loves books and education.
- Mark Brooks of Cianbro loves leadership and military history.

- Jas Sekhon of Bluegrass ADD loves business development and golf.
- Jim Theriault of Cianbro loves history and church.
- Dan Gregorie of Choicecare loves boats and travel.
- Dave Richeson of Stabilus loves his family and dogs.
- Fred Link of Deep Cove loves leadership and learning.
- Terri Swanson of Swanson Associates loves people and travel.
- Steve Bailey of Maine School Management loves education and the ocean
- Cyndy Miller of FAA loves people and books.
- John Rees of CCA loves innovation and corrections management.
- Gerald Hunter of Norfolk State University loves basketball and cigars.
- Carl Stenberg of UNC-Chapel Hill loves racing cars and golf.
- Susan Wehrspann of the University of Colorado Health loves photography and singing.
- Angie Woodward of Leadership Kentucky loves cars and education.
- Bob Caplon of IBM loves learning and volunteering.
- Mendy Blair of Baptist Health loves education and healthcare.
- Bill Harwood of the Maine State Police loves law enforcement and leadership.

It helps to know the personal interests and enjoyments of clients, such as sports, nature, music, travel, etc., in addition to family, church, country, and other values. Getting to know each other builds trust and loyalty between people, the bedrocks of satisfying and productive relationships.

Lesson: Rhode Island writer H. P. Lovecraft makes the point that we are all unique, noting that *home* is the universal haven of the odd, dissenting and free ... where they have to take you in.

#47

No Turtle Ever Got on a Fencepost by Itself – Staff Support

Every consultant needs a good accountant and a great secretary. These are force-multipliers for success. I've been enormously fortunate to have competent and reliable assistance for over 52 years. Beginning in 1970, accounting was done by Cliff Stone for 20 years, Cathy Wasson for 15 years, and Roy Dorsey for 17 years. Keeping complete and accurate financial records saves enormous amounts of time, worry, and money. Secretarial support was provided by Irene Brownfield for 2 years, Linda Williams for 6 years, Kathy Lyons for 6 years, Pam Pfaff for 3 years, and Barb Thomes for 35 years. A developmental task I never accomplished was legible handwriting. My writing became harder to read with each year and is now nearly illegible. The patience and accommodation of those who have been willing to try to decipher my writing is appreciated beyond words, especially when typing manuscripts. Jennifer Futrell and Lindsey Walker have helped prepare books and blogs for seven years. **Lesson Learned: No turtle ever got on a fencepost by itself.**

It's important to note that some successful consultants operate like a one-person shop, doing most of the administrative work (accounting and secretarial) personally. The value of this is less cost; the negative is less time for providing consulting services. It's also important to note the increasing role of the internet in providing staff support. Not everybody has to work in the same location. My support includes legal, accounting, technology, and publishing support from eight states – California, Colorado, Illinois, Iowa, Kentucky, Ohio, Maine, and Tennessee.

#48

Diversity as a Strength

As a professor and consultant, I have witnessed the benefits of diversity. Native Americans, Asians, Hispanics, African Americans, Europeans, and a host of other people have made America a kaleidoscope of good and talented people with unique perspectives and gifts. For example, five Indians from India have proven this to me – 3 professors and 2 clients. I have known these individuals as friends since the early 1970s and have watched them serve their fellow Americans for over 50 years: Jas Sekhon, a government leader/planner; Jiten Shah, a government leader/engineer; Tripta Desai, a world history professor; Vinay Kumar, a chemistry professor; and Yudister Datta, an accounting professor. They have raised their families in America and love the land of the free and the home of the brave with all of their hearts. Three years ago, our university selected an Indian President, Ashish Vaidya, who loves and serves the university as much as any Kentuckian, Buckeye, or Hoosier native could. Diversity is more than a theory or something to read about when you look around and see the good it brings to society and the individual. **Lesson learned: celebrate the common goodness in all people and the special perspectives and talents of diverse people.**

#49

The Balance of Theory and Practice

Theory and practice are both important in consulting. Kurt Lewin, the father of social psychology, thought *there is nothing more practical than a good theory,* and William James, the father of American psychology, thought *theory is useless unless it's based on reality.* Being a professor helps my consulting to be theoretically sound for clients. Being a consultant helps my teaching to be interesting and useful for students.

Lesson learned: Both teaching and consulting are other-serving activities. If you are truly learner-centered, you will be a successful professor. If you are truly client-focused, you will be a successful consultant. Combining teaching and consulting has been a good fit for me. Philosophically, I value bridging the gap between theory and practice, between classroom and job, between school and work.

The main thing about teaching is the responsibility you feel toward student learning. It's truer than not: if the learner hasn't learned, the teacher hasn't taught. The main thing about consulting is the value you bring to the client. Is your service useful? Does it prevent or solve problems? Does it add value? The consultant must feel responsible to serve the client well.

Both teaching and consulting require good planning. The planning document for teaching is the syllabus. It provides the structure, content, and processes of a course, including the course description, instructor responsibilities, student requirements, learning resources, methods of instruction, methods of evaluation, grading standards, schedule of activities, and an ethics clause. The professor gives the syllabus life to make sure student learning is achieved.

The planning document for consulting is the consulting agreement. It answers the question of who is responsible for doing what by when, where, how, and why, including the schedule and amount of payment for satisfactory service, as well as an ethics clause. The consultant gives the agreement life to make sure good results are achieved for the client.

As a professor, I make sure the best text and learning materials are used. These will be the backbone of the course, and I tailor the schedule and activities based on these. For example, when I taught Principles of Economics, 1970-73, I used Paul Samuelson's *Economics*, first published in 1948 and now in its 19th edition. Samuelson was the first American to win the Nobel Prize in Economics. I complemented this text with Robert Heilbroner's reader, *The Worldly Philosophers: The Lives, Times, and Ideas of The Great Economic Thinker*s, to humanize what Thomas Carlyle called the 'dismal science.' Students were tested on the content of these books and were graded for mastery.

As a consultant, I make sure the best methods and tools are used to achieve the best outcomes. I tailor these to the task at hand. I do this primarily by reading extensively, starting with the foundational literature on a subject (morale, performance, leadership, motivation, ethics, communication, quality, stress, etc.). I add contemporary books, articles, and talks to stay current. As a consultant, I'm guided by a 4-P mantra – poor planning results in poor performance, so I spend the time needed to properly plan and prepare. I think in pictures, and if I can picture a completed project with good outcomes, I work to make it happen.

#50

Managing Human Capital

The research and findings of the Gallup organization have helped focus my efforts on the human side of work, including the areas of employee retention and managing human capital. Gallup identifies four strategies that combine to achieve up to 59 percent more growth in revenue per employee: 1. First, select managers with leadership ability at all levels of the organization. When companies have good managers, they can achieve 27 percent higher revenue per employee than average. 2. Second, select the right employees. Hire employees who have integrity, initiative, and intelligence for the job they are doing. The additive effect of selecting good employees can be 6 percent higher revenue per employee. 3. Third, engage employees. This means being sure employees can answer yes to Gallup questions that predict employee engagement.

Six questions with strong links to positive business outcomes are: Do I know what is expected of me at work? Do I have the materials and equipment I need to do my best work? At work, do I have the opportunity to do what I do best every day? In the last seven days, have I received recognition or praise for doing good work? Does my supervisor, or someone at work, seem to care about me as a person? Is there someone at work who encourages my development? The additive effect of engaged employees can be 18 percent higher revenue per employee. 4. Fourth, focus on employee strengths. It reduces apathy, anxiety, and boredom when they are challenged to do what they are good at doing. The additive effect can be 8 percent higher revenue per employee. When companies implement these four strategies, they maximize the potential of their human capital with a combined effect of up to 59 percent more revenue per employee. Government and not-for-profit organizations can expect the same performance improvements.

Consulting message: Clients expect consultants to be aware of current information and empirical data. The Gallup organization is a trusted partner in providing accurate and useful survey information. Helping clients in the areas of leadership selection and development, recruitment and development of employees, creating a healthy and productive work culture, and coaching people to succeed has been satisfying and rewarding.

#51

Technology Challenges

From the beginning, I've used handouts and visual aids to support university classes and consulting lectures, seminars, and workshops. In 1966, I started out with a blackboard and white chalk; today, I use PowerPoints and internet videos. In between, I used a green board and yellow chalk, flip charts and magic markers, overhead transparencies, 16 mm films, 35 mm slide trays, 3/4 inch and 1/2 videotapes, and DVDs. Every shift to a new technology has been a great challenge and has nearly shut me down. I have always been a low-tech person and a late adopter to changes in instructional methods and tools. Machines, tools, and instruments have been barriers for me ever since I was a boy. I have no interest or aptitude in the mechanical world. If I had been born in ancient Greece, drawing on clay tablets would have been fine.

To this day, I don't understand physics or chemistry, even though I received an A in both courses (I memorized the material for the moment). I can't change the oil in my car, and levers, dials, switches, and buttons are a mystery. I'm not against new methods and technologies, such as online learning; it's just that adjusting to these technologies has been a big challenge. I don't have an attitude problem so much as a skill problem. I would be cooked without the help of understanding and patient people who are willing to help me make difficult transitions. Our university media department has been fantastic, the staff at McGraw-Hill has been outstanding, and many caring and competent students and clients have helped me survive technological challenges. **Lesson learned: One must keep up with changes in the cyber world to be an effective consultant. This includes proficiency in the use of computers and phones. Adapting to ongoing technological change requires having skilled partners.**

An increasing trend is providing online consulting services. This works particularly well in the area of coaching where the service is often the same – advice provided from the head and heart – with less expense. A great leap for me has been online podcasts, interviews, and seminars. A leap, yes; great, I'm not sure. Nothing beats face-to-face human interaction. What I know is I'm 'leaning into' new ways of consulting and teaching and will give it my best effort. So far, clients include private businesses, government agencies, and non-profit organizations. As for the future, who can say? There is a saying that man plans, God laughs. AI and holograms are adjustments ahead. **In any case, the successful consultant must be eternal in principle and agile in delivery.**

#52

The Theory and Practice of Leadership – Balance is Best

Many of my consulting projects involve leadership development, including speeches, seminars, and coaching. Google conducted a study called Project Oxygen that showed good leadership is essential for company success. The study revealed 8 leadership behaviors that were like breaths of fresh air: empowering others, coaching to succeed, communicating a vision, showing concern for others, being results-oriented, focusing on career development, being an effective communicator, and having technical skills. To develop leaders, Google provides Oxygen 8 panel discussions with its best managers. Engineers who avoid theories and lectures are willing to listen to practical advice from engineering managers they respect. I find this to be the case in all fields of work.

Lesson: Presentations on the theory and practice of leadership are most popular and helpful when I provide the theory and a highly respected leader in the field shares personal experience, practical application, and useful advice to the audience. It's especially helpful when leaders share mistakes they have made and what they learned from them. I've done this in the following industries and professions: manufacturing, construction, medicine, transportation, education, hospitality, criminal justice, retail, financial services, energy, and the military. Participants listen politely when I talk, but they listen intently when a leader they respect shares what they know and do.

#53

Problem Solving and Human Relations – Two Magic Keys (The Skeleton Key/ The Master Key)

The essence of management consulting is solving problems, and most problems involve people. When a client has a problem, I say thank goodness you recognize it, because the problems you deny and those you don't address are the ones that will do you in. Problems are often complex, so simplicity is needed. In 1979, I developed two useful keys that are easy to remember – The Skeleton Key and the Master Key.

The Skeleton Key for solving problems has four steps:

Step 1. Get the facts. As Mark Twain said, "Get the facts first; then you can distort them as much as you please." You can't solve a problem without first knowing the facts, so (a) review all records, (b) talk with the people concerned, (c) consider opinions and feelings, and (d) look at all sides. Keep an open mind, unlike some minds that are like concrete, thoroughly mixed up and permanently set.

Step 2. Weigh and decide. After getting the facts, weigh each fact against the others, fit the pieces together, and consider alternatives. Consider the effects that different decisions will have on individuals and groups. Sometimes it's a good idea to sleep on a problem so that you don't jump to conclusions or overreact.

Step 3. Take action. After you've gathered the facts and determined a course of action, carry out your plan. Harry Truman realized the importance of this step when he said, "The buck stops here," and "If you can't stand the heat, get out of the kitchen."

Step 4. Follow up and ask: did my action help the quality of work or the quality of work-life? If not, find a better solution. By taking time to follow up on actions and being willing to admit mistakes, you achieve three important goals: (a) the respect of all who are watching, (b) another chance to solve the problem, and (c) the opportunity to set an example of honesty and thoroughness in problem-solving.

Abraham Lincoln used this four-step sequence in solving problems. He began by gathering all the facts, often by going to the battlefield to get the facts personally. Then he weighed possible solutions and the consequences of each, encouraging suggestions from a wide array of people and perspectives. Then he took decisive action consistent with his values and policy objectives. Finally, he followed up to see if his decision advanced his two abiding goals: preserving the union and abolishing slavery. If it's good enough for Abraham Lincoln in the Civil War, It's good enough for us today.

The Master Key for human relations has four principles:

Principle 1. Let people know where they stand. You should communicate expectations and keep people informed on how they are doing. If criticism is necessary, do it in private; if praise is in order, give it in public.

Principle 2. Give credit where it's due. Look for extra or unusual performance and show appreciation as soon as possible. As a rule, the greatest credit should be given to those who try the hardest, sacrifice the most, and perform the most difficult work.

Principle 3. Tell people as soon as possible about decisions that will affect them. Keep people informed and tell them why a decision is necessary.

Principle 4. Make the best use of each person's ability. Let each person shine as only that person can. Everyone is gifted, but most people never open their package. Take the time to look for potential not now being used.

University President James Votruba provides useful advice about solving problems and making decisions with moral consequences. For every decision you make, project out five steps and ask if your action is taking you in the direction you want to go. Also, when faced with two negative courses of action, think about which decision is easier for your conscience to live with. **Lesson: The Skeleton and Master keys are beautiful in their simplicity and have helped me greatly as a consultant. Both are easy to remember, easy to use, and are always effective. Another message is the importance of involving the client for a lasting impact. Client understanding, ownership, and effectiveness increase in proportion to personal involvement.**

#54

Murphy's Law

I don't know who said it or where I heard it first, but Murphy's 1st Law is, "Anything that can go wrong will." The 2nd Law is, "Nothing is as easy as it looks." The 3rd Law is, "Everything takes longer than you think it will." The experienced consultant is familiar with these laws. Regarding Murphy's 1st Law, a consultant must be ready for the unexpected. You must picture and plan for the best, but be prepared for the worst.

I always have a backup plan and built-in redundancy. I prepare for the unexpected as much as possible when serving a client. To do this, I use a preparation checklist and a mental tour of the upcoming event, imagining what could go wrong and the best way to handle it – much like a captain of a ship or plane. Weather, equipment, and human factors can derail plans, so think ahead and have a plan B. It's sometimes good to envision even a plan C.

If you are flying, use direct flights when possible. Schedule the earliest flight and have backup flights or methods of transportation. Keep your car in excellent working order with emergency tools handy and have a spare key in your wallet. Keep important information and equipment you will need with you. Be on guard against loss or theft. Pay attention to details and don't let your mind wander. If you could have prevented a problem such as running out of gas, missing a flight, or forgetting an important document, the client's disappointment will be real, and trust will be lost. Some examples of the unexpected – two preventable, three not:

1. *Serving Texoma Medical Center (Ron Seal)* – I let my mind wander at the Dallas airport and left my briefcase and planner sitting on the bench when the rental car bus picked me up. When I returned 45 minutes later, both the briefcase and planner were still on the bench. I would have been cooked without these materials – my own fault and preventable.

2. *Serving the Indiana Department of Corrections (Dan Ronay)* – I left my computer in the hotel room and it was gone when I returned from getting coffee in the lobby. I didn't close the hotel room door completely and this made doing a project more difficult – my own fault and preventable.

3. *Serving Cianbro Industries (Pat Hinckley)* – A snowstorm knocked out power in Portland. Plan B was to convene the group at the Eastland Hotel and conduct the class in the lobby (without power) – not preventable.

4. *Serving the Florida Department of Corrections (Ed Buss)* – A hurricane required the cancellation of an All-Warden conference to ensure personal safety and the security of institutions – not preventable.

5. ***Serving the Bank of Oklahoma (Chris Gausvik)*** – Wind prevented landing in Tulsa the evening before an all-day event with the Bank of Oklahoma. The closest safe landing was at Wichita requiring an all-night drive in a storm – not preventable.

Early in my consulting career, I read Robert Burns' famous quotation: "The best-laid plans of mice and men often go astray." I've read that the original eighteenth century Scots version was "The best laid schemes o' mice an' men Gang aft a-gley," but we'll stick with our modern translation. And it aptly expresses something that's true no matter how well one plans and prepares. By the middle of my career, I knew people were like teabags: you don't know what they are made of until you put them in hot water. **Lesson: The successful consultant is a super teabag with a can-do spirit and a 'whatever it takes' attitude. The client hopes the consultant will plan and prepare thoroughly and will not make preventable mistakes of either omission or commission; and will handle unpreventable problems and emergencies calmly and intelligently. A saying that originated in England during World War II gives good guidance – keep calm and carry on. Do this, and clients will love it.**

#55

Maine Projects and Activities

Most consulting can be traced from something to something including a touch of luck and good timing. It's satisfying and brings a smile. For example, I first met the management team of 'Cianbro' in 2002 at a leadership retreat held at *Inn by The Sea* in Cape Elizabeth, Maine. This was traced to a talk I had given for the Maine Development Foundation at the *Samoset Resort* in Rockland, Maine in 2001.

Kellie Guarino was the coordinator of the MDF event and relied on the advice of Angie Woodward who had created Leadership Kentucky, a national model for statewide leadership development. Leadership Kentucky was a year-long program with a class of 50 Kentucky leaders from the private, public, and nonprofit sectors each year. Meeting locations included: a coal mine, horse farm, bourbon distillery, riverboat, Fort Knox, Mammoth Cave, Lake Cumberland, Churchill Downs, and the State Capitol. I provided the opening session on 'Building Community,' a mid-session on 'Caring Leadership,' and the closing session on 'Leading Change' each year. Leadership Kentucky was traced to a planning retreat I had with the Cabinet of Kentucky Governor Martha Layne Collins . . . and so on, backward.

Going forward, Cianbro's endorsement led to relationships with additional Maine clients – Bangor Savings Bank (Jim Dow), Jackson Laboratory (Rick Woychik), Maine Department of Education (Susan Berry and Steve Bailey), and Maine State Police (Bill Harwood, Jim Theriault, David Tripp). Similarly, consulting with EMERA Energy (Bob Hanf) came from the recommendation of American Electric Power (Brian Tierney), Northern Light Health (Gavin Ducker) came from the Health Alliance (Jack Cook) and Tri-Health (Claus Von Zychlin) Systems in Cincinnati, Casco Bay Convention & Visitors Bureau (Lynn Tillotson) came from the International Association of Convention & Visitor Bureaus (Joe McGrath), Martin's Point Health Care (David Howes) came from Humana-Choicecare (Dan Gregorie), VHA New England (Bill Vanderburg) came from University of Louisville Health (James Taylor), Maine Public Broadcasting Network (Jim Dow) came from the American Financial Group (Dan Keefe), and Witham Family Hotels (Fred Link and Terri Swanson) came from Commonwealth Hotels (Dan Fay and Gordy Snyder). **The lesson I learned is the importance of word-of-mouth recommendations from respected people. This is especially the case when consulting services impact a client's health, wealth, and reputation. In the final analysis, consulting is based on trusting relationships that are built over time – client by client, service by service.**

Maine projects and activities include: The Maine Development Foundation (leadership summit); The Cianbro Companies (sustaining culture through leadership development); VHA New England (leadership development/affinity groups); Martin's Point Health Care (physician leadership/organization development); Casco Bay Convention and Visitors Bureau (the human side of hospitality); Bangor Savings Bank (new leadership development); The Jackson Laboratory (building community – working together effectively); EMERA Energy (management development/leading change); Maine Public Broadcasting Network (professional development); Witham Family Hotels (positive work culture); Northern Light Health (physician leadership development); Maine School Management Association (positive work culture) Maine State Police (leadership development); and Nate Holyoke Builders (leadership development). The variety is gratifying and always extends my own continuing education.

In his work on servant leadership, management author Robert Greenleaf proposed that the world could be saved as long as three truly great organizations exist – one in the private sector, one in the public sector, and one in the nonprofit sector. He thought these organizations would be beacons of light and that their success could be traced to caring leadership and the empowerment of people. The Cianbro Companies is an organization that has fulfilled this role in the private sector. The culture of Cianbro is based on four statements: 1. It's all about people; 2. None of us is as smart as all of us; 3. Never say can't; and 4. Your word is your bond.

Other values are important at Cianbro, such as being innovative and working lean, but these four values best define the company. Cianbro makes hard work satisfying because they are like the Marines and will tackle anything – tunnels, bridges, and structures of any kind and size. The four Cianchette brothers started with a truck, a shovel, and a wheelbarrow. Cianbro is now a billion-dollar employee-owned company with over four thousand team members operating in forty states. I've had the opportunity to serve the Cianbro Corporation in the area of leadership development for over 20 years. What an honor!

#56

A Nod to Freud

A nod to Freud – Freud thought early experiences were important determinants of behavior. For example, if a little girl gets attention from her father by acting cute and feminine, she is likely to behave the same way with male figures all of her life. If a little boy has trouble dealing with his authoritarian father, it's likely to influence his behavior with future male authorities in the classroom, military, and work environment.

A quick snapshot of my growing up years: I had a happy childhood growing up in Middletown, Ohio. I was an only child with a slew of cousins from a total of 27 aunts and uncles. My Mom was a homemaker, and my dad was a breadwinner. She was loving and supportive and he was strong and demanding. We were a classic middle-class family. My dad was the protector (when I was eight years old, he killed a snake on a trail that I will never forget); my mom was the nurturer (Freud thought that boys who felt loved by their mothers were forever blessed with feelings of importance).

I was greatly influenced by the Baptist church, public schools, Boy Scouts, YMCA, summer camp, family vacations, holiday celebrations, and neighborhood playmates. My best two friends were Roy Biggs and Dick West. I loved playing baseball and basketball. My biggest problem was body image – being heavy from six through 12. It was traumatic when my mom took me to the Central store and asked, "where's the husky department?"

Mark Twain said, "Be yourself . . . everyone else is taken." I learned to do this in my growing-up years. I knew I liked sports and books and didn't like fishing. I knew I had little mechanical ability but loved Old Radio. I knew I didn't like clutter, was my own decider, and needed to feel free. I knew I was against prejudice and cruelty and believed in kindness. I knew I was for goodness but had gaps. I knew I was physically clumsy, mentally spacey, and accident-prone. Finally, I knew I was an optimist . . . I might not know exactly where I'm going, but I'm happily on my way. I buy in fully to the positive example of Abraham Lincoln who thought if you think you can, you can; if you think you can't, you're right. These are all still true and not likely to change.

Does age matter? Yes and no. Age brings experience and perspective that can change behavior, including judgment; but the core personality tends to be constant. **Lesson: Every person has a unique personality that deep down is not likely to change. Consulting success requires flexibility to understand, appreciate, and deal effectively with a wide variety of people.**

#57

My Best Two Leaders

Ralph Tesseneer and Vince Schulte were the best two leaders I have ever had. Our styles of work were different, but our values were the same. Ralph and Vince accommodated my need for independence, and I was responsive to their needs for order and reliability. Above all, these were men of integrity and courage. In any dilemma, their first concern was for the student, then the faculty, and their own interests were never considered. It's safe to say that without their encouragement and support, I couldn't have been an effective professor and consultant. Beginning in 1970, Ralph and Vince saw the value of combining the world of teaching with the world of work. Leaders thereafter continued this support for me, thank goodness. **Lesson: Ralph and Vince validated my belief that caring about the work and caring about people were the two essential requirements for effective leadership. In addition, they had integrity, job knowledge, and people-building skills. They were the gold standard on all counts.**

#58

How Writing Helps Consulting and Vice-Versa

Most consultants write – letters, reports, articles, and books. It could be argued that every adult should write something, even if it's not required in one's work. Much good comes from writing, including self-discipline, focused thought, sharing the content of one's reflections, and personal satisfaction. Writing can be personal, such as a family history, or it can be professional, such as a paper in one's field of expertise. My first writing was a maintenance manual and staff handbook for a country club swimming pool when I was 17. I learned five writing rules that helped me as a consultant 10 years later and to this day: **1. Write what you know about; 2. Write the way you talk; 3. Write, read, and re-write for clarity; 4. Proof for errors, including spelling; 5. Write logically.** A useful technique for consulting documents is to be sure you answer the questions who, what, why, when, where, and how clearly and succinctly. This is greatly appreciated by clients.

The following publications have helped my consulting career: *The Human Side of Work* series; *Building Community*; *Stress: Living* and *Working in a Changing World*; *The Art of Leadership*; and *Leadership Today*.

a. The Human Side of Work series (hotels, beaches and airplanes)

From 1970 to 1977, I was so busy with family, teaching, and consulting activities that there was no time for anything else. Then, our Dean, Joe Price, told me I received a sabbatical to write *The Human Side of Work* series. My goal was to write what I had learned from good theorists and researchers so future professors and practitioners could use this material. I used a yellow pad and pencil and wrote for six months.

I wrote about 15 subjects and arranged these into eight volumes that would become *The Human Side of Work* series – Morale, Performance, Leadership, Ethics, Human Behavior, Communication, Quality, and Stress. Each book in the series stood alone and included theory, practice, related articles, and exercises to teach the subject. My friend and co-author Kent Curtis added practical perspective and current research to every book. The books were like popcorn for professors and consultants who could mix and match the contents to meet the needs of students and clients. Under the guidance of editor Stan DeMille, the content was strong. Under the guidance of Harold Utly, the books were well-received. South-Western Publishing sold a ton. *The Human Side of Work* series was started in 1980 and published in 1988, based on a book each year. In 1982, Prentice-Hall offered a contract for the series, but the pressure of a publishing contract on top of home, school, and consulting was over-stressful. Signing a contract with South-Western Publishing in 1987 with all drafts completed was better for peace of mind. *The Human Side of Work* series was written for college courses, but the books proved to be equally popular in corporate and government markets.

b. Building Community (the St. John Six)

Because *The Human Side of Work series* sold well, South-Western Publishing (later Thomson Learning, now Cengage Learning) asked for three books that would fit an 'executive press' audience including business schools and leaders. *Building community* was started in 1993 and was published in 1996. There are two ways to experience community at work – by bringing people together in place and time, and by lowering barriers between people so that the culture is strong and good work is done. *Building Community* was highly useful as a resource for developing and sustaining communication, teamwork, and a one-team attitude. It was a popular book for courses in group dynamics and organizational development. I completed the final edits of the book on St. John Island in the Caribbean Sea. The beach cove I used was like a picture postcard of rare and magnificent beauty. The last day there showed why when six nude figures were unexpectedly cavorting on the sand. I averted my gaze and finished my task. *Building Community* was a memorable book. This has been a useful book for me in the areas of visioning, team building, and creating a healthy work culture.

c. Stress: Living and Working in a Changing World (Puerto Rico)

Stress: Living and Working in a Changing World was started in 1996 and completed in Puerto Rico in 1999. It's a comprehensive book on the subject of stress, beginning with stress physiology and ending with healthy behaviors. Chapters address personality and stress, stress across the lifespan, personal stress, interpersonal stress, stress in the workplace, and peak performance. The book is written for three audiences: 1. College and university courses; 2. Individuals and organizations helping people manage stress; 3. Overworked and overstressed individuals seeking personal wellbeing. The first edition was published by Whole Person Press – Carlene Sippola and Susan Gustafson; the second edition was published by Savant Learning – Kevin Warren and Susan Rubendall; the third edition was also published by Savant Learning – Kevin Warren and Jennifer Futrell Zimmerman.

The Father of Stress Management is Hans Selye who recommends timeless advice: 1. Regardless of how much you want to be loved, it's useless to try to befriend someone who continuously rejects you. 2. Face the fact that there is no such thing as perfection. Your highest goal is to be the best you can be. 3. Returning to a simpler lifestyle can add more pleasure to life than all the wealth and extravagance you've been struggling to obtain. 4. Before you waste a lot of energy trying to fight your way out of a situation, ask yourself, is it really worth fighting for? 5. Focus only on what is good in your life, forgetting anything painful or ugly. 6. When you face your most difficult hour, try to recall and dwell on a past success. A sense of frustration can totally immobilize you. You can avoid this by concentrating on even the slightest bright spot in your past. 7. Never detour from unpleasant tasks. Face them as soon as possible so that you can move on to more enjoyable things. 8. There are no pat answers or special formulas for success that will fit everyone. Choose from a wide variety of advice only those things that fit your own unique personality. I had no idea how much demand would grow for consulting in leading change and managing stress, increasing every year since 1980.

d. *The Art of Leadership (home in Maine)*

Seven editions of *The Art of Leadership* have been published by McGraw-Hill between 2002 and 2022. I associate this book with Nancy, so it's a favorite. I would stretch out books and drafts on a card table beside Nancy and we would lose track of time. Publisher John Biernat acquired the book in 2002 and Andy Winston edited the first edition. Laura Spell and Mike Ablassmeir have been champions of *The Art of Leadership* for courses and programs throughout the world. This is a comprehensive text on leadership development with nine parts – Leadership Variables, The Power of Vision, The Importance of Ethics, The Empowerment of People, Leadership Principles, Understanding People, Multiplying Effectiveness, Developing Others, and Performance Management. The audience for *The Art of Leadership* is both new and experienced leaders. Writing the book has kept me current as a professor and consultant. It bridges the gap between school and work and between theory and practice like no other endeavor. It's especially useful as courseware for leadership education and as a desk book for leadership coaching. I often provide train-the-trainer consulting for organizations using the book for leadership development.

e. *Leadership Today (blogs)*

In 2021, McGraw-Hill developed a **Leadership Today** webpage for *The Art of Leadership* text. It has blogs on leadership subjects ranging from servant leadership to leadership ethics, including leading quality, leading change, transformational leadership, the diversity challenge, and adaptive capacity. It also has podcasts including managing personal and professional stress. These blogs and podcasts are useful as pre-read, class discussion, and after-class assignments. I've enjoyed working with the creative team at McGraw-Hill to produce these 'thought pieces' – Lindsey Walker, Debbie Clare, Amelia Hurd, Hannah MacNaughton, Hannah Kusper, Lisa Granger, and Karryn Vogt. They put zip and meaning in the words, "Never a dull moment, Oh My!"

Writing lesson: I learned to write in variable chunks of time and in unusual places. I would block out time from one hour to 12 hours and fit this around family, teaching, and consulting responsibilities. Although I preferred writing at home, I had to

be flexible. I would write wherever I could, including planes, diners, beaches, and libraries. If I had paper, pencil, and time, I could make meaningful progress wherever I was. You are meant to write if time stands still when you do.

#59

The Red River Leadership Institute – The Strength of a Region (Building Community Without Losing Culture)

The Red River Leadership Institute is the brainchild of Jim Youngquist and his colleagues in the four-state region encompassing Arkansas, Louisiana, Oklahoma, and Texas. In 2019 - 2020, a regional leadership development program was coordinated by the University of Arkansas. Participants were public sector government leaders, private sector business leaders, and non-profit sector community leaders. There were three goals: Serve the Red River Region by advancing talent, technology, and tolerance (3Ts); Build leadership skills that will enhance the region including participating organizations; Develop professional relationships to form networks of influence that will sustain the growth and wellbeing of the region. The Red River Leadership Institute initiative was a success on all counts: new and productive relationships were formed among 25 participants; leadership skills were honed for both emerging and experienced leaders; sub-groups worked together to improve the Red River Region in four areas – developing regional commercial hot spots in addition to New Orleans and Austin; reducing government bureaucracy and regulations that hinder the economic development of the region; strengthening the regional social fabric without losing the traditional and unique character of diverse groups in the Red River region; Improving healthcare access throughout the four-state region, including sparsely populated areas.

The Red River Leadership Institute goes forward led by Mary Beth Rudel and the Red River Institute advisory board. Reinforced by success, the goals are continued development of talent, technology, and tolerance in the region, development of leadership skills for a new cohort of participants and their organizations, and development of lasting relationships among regional leaders. My role as a consultant is to provide leadership development and facilitate teamwork in six leadership workshops spread over the year-long project. Participants will use the 7th edition of *The Art of Leadership* as courseware. **Lessons learned: leaders from private businesses, government agencies, and non-profit organizations admire each other and enjoy working together to strengthen their region. Learning, working, and serving together is satisfying and results in meaningful accomplishments.**

#60

Golf Course Pearls – Make Your Last Work Your Best Work

As the story goes, Clint Eastwood and Toby Keith were playing golf and Clint said he was going to shoot a new movie. Toby asked how he kept so strong and current. Clint was 88 years old at the time. What was his secret? Clint said, "I wake up in the morning and don't let the old man in." Toby went home and wrote the title song for Eastwood's movie, *The Mule*. The lessons of this story have stuck with me: 1. Don't let the old man in. 2. Strive to make your last work your best work. 3. Collaborate across generations and disciplines to make the best results. 4. Leave this world all worn out doing what you are meant to do. **Lesson: Have an exit philosophy for your life and work. And as long as you work, don't let the old man in.**

#61

Don't Take Yourself Too Seriously

Humility is a consulting asset, in contrast to arrogance, which is a liability. Although clients want you to be knowledgeable and current, if you come across as a know-it-all, they will view you as self-centered and ego-striving, and they will avoid you. The answer is, "Don't take yourself too seriously . . . no one else does." **Lesson: Take your work seriously, but don't exaggerate your importance. A little humility goes a long way.**

#62

Coping With Change – The Path of a Book

Charles Darwin said: It is not the strongest of the species that survive, nor the most intelligent, but the one most responsive to change. Truer words were never spoken. I used to think that change would happen everywhere except in universities. Time proved this to be wrong. From what is taught to how it's taught, higher education has changed, and I've had to adjust or go the way of the dinosaur, which is extinction. For example, writing a book used to be simple – a yellow pencil, a pad of paper, and a good typist. Computers and word processing changed all of that, as publishing the seventh edition of *The Art of Leadership* shows: written in Maine, acquired in New York, managed in Chicago, developed in Iowa, designed in India, copy-edited in Greece, proofed in Ireland, art in California, printed in Canada, Instructor's Guide in North Carolina.

Regarding teaching online, it's a challenge I could never have imagined. The downside is the loss of learning that occurs without face-to-face interactions in the classroom. The upside is access to learning from anywhere in the world, including the opportunity to address individual questions much more deeply. Around twenty-five hundred years ago, the philosopher Heraclitus said, "Things are always changing." He was right. **Lessons: There are two myths about change – 1. Change will go away, when the truth is that change is here to stay. 2. You can just keep on doing what you have been doing, when the truth is that if your world is changing, you will have to change as well.** Personally, with help, I can adjust, but I would rather use a pencil and teach in a classroom.

#63

Career Advice – Straight Shots, Zig Zags, and Loop Arounds

When I started teaching in 1966, I thought the best path to success was the straightest path, and that was my advice to young people. Any time off this path was a detriment to career success and life satisfaction. As the years have passed and I've listened to the stories of many students, I've concluded there is no single path to success. Ups and downs, detours, and circle backs can be highly educational and valuable. The key is what you learn and do on your own unique journey. **I've learned three lessons: 1. To get what you've never had, you must do what you've never done – be open; 2. Tenacity is easier when you have no choice – persist; 3. Life is not measured by the number of breaths we take, but by the moments that take our breath away – say yes.** My advice for young people today is to explore the world with an open mind, pursue your dreams with guts and grit, and when opportunity knocks-answer.

It's said that the shape of one's face in the first half of life determines the shape of one's face in the second half of life; frowns freeze and smiles please. In a similar way, what you do before your middle years determines the quality of your life in your later years. **The young consultant should strive to accomplish these six tasks: 1. Know yourself – know who you are and what is important to you; 2. Become an expert – develop knowledge and skills people need and will pay you to do; 3. Establish your style – work in a manner that is both comfortable and productive; 4. Build a network – be generous and helpful in service to others; 5. Create a cushion – for every dollar earned, invest a percentage for economic security; 6. Be true to your values – integrity is the indispensable element of consulting success. The importance of number six is supported by Oliver Wendell Holmes, Jr.: What lies behind us and what lies before us are tiny compared to what lies within us.**

#64

Handling Stressful Situations

Consultants are often in stressful situations. You must not panic and must not freeze. You must focus on the task, think clearly, and act decisively. Three points to remember: 1. You have to provide a solution to the problem; 2. Everyone is watching you to see how you handle the situation; 3. You don't want to have a stroke. A good example sticks in my mind: In 1998, St. Luke Hospital CEO Nancy Barone was attending a Christmas dinner and celebration for all hospital employees. There was a commotion in the back of the room where an employee had collapsed in the men's room. Barone, who was a nurse, quickly, quietly, and personally addressed the emergency and saved the man's life. **Lesson: In this stressful situation, she focused, thought, and acted.** Only a few people knew there was a crisis. Nancy Barone became a successful international consultant in health care leadership and remains a role model in staying calm and handling emergencies.

#65

Unexpected Loss and the Phoenix Phenomenon – From Overhead Projector to Flash Drive

    Like a phoenix, the Egyptian mythical bird that perished by fire and then rose from the ashes to live another day, the consultant must be resilient and recover from inevitable setbacks. After Nancy's stroke in 1990, my most stressful experience was in 2002 when my car was broken into and everything leather was stolen – a planner filled with life and work commitments and detailed records, and a large briefcase containing all the resources I use for teaching courses and doing consulting. It was 6:00 am on a Wednesday and I was scheduled to give a 7:00 am talk at Bethesda Hospital on either ethics or stress. I didn't know which, but I had no notes in either case. I had class at 9:00 am at the university but didn't know the subject and activities without my planner. I had to fly to Washington the next morning, but I didn't know the time without my planner and didn't have the ticket that was in the planner pocket. Critically, the subjects I taught were all supported by overhead transparencies and handouts in the briefcase that was now gone forever. My checkbook, passport, and health records were gone.

A police report was filed, and an investigation was conducted, but nothing was found.

Immediately, I faced four giant problems: 1. Reconstructing the syllabus, lesson plans, and handouts for four courses. 2. Reconstructing a year-ahead calendar and schedule of client engagements and travel details, including important notes. 3. Recreating the content of overhead transparencies into PowerPoint slides for classes and speeches. 4. Replacing personal records and family information – birth and marriage certificates, passport, health records, insurance cards, bank book, checks, and financial details. With the help of caring colleagues, these challenges were met, thank goodness. I wish I could say we caught the culprit when he kept showing up for my speeches and consulting engagements with very good overhead transparencies and notes. But alas, neither of us was able to make use of all those treasures again.

Lessons learned: 1. Keep backup files for courses and clients. 2. Lock all home, car, and office doors. 3. I couldn't recover from these losses without the help of patient students, understanding clients, and helpful colleagues. 4. Avoid crashes but be like the phoenix as all consultants must rise again.

Conclusion

I've been up late writing these stories. I don't know why. It seemed to fit – being alone, happy reflections, sharing lessons. I'm finished now, so final thoughts: The end of a book is the chance to say thank you to readers and share last thoughts. Psychologist David Alter reports: Deep beneath the streets of Rome sits the Capuchin Crypt, a catacomb housing the bones of nearly 4,000 monks. An inscription on the wall reads, "What you are now we used to be; what we are now you will be." Can it be said more starkly? We are mortal and our lives will end one day. So, how do we want to live our lives during the all too short time we have? My family needs a library, but this short book is a summary of what I have learned from my professional life.

Eleanor Roosevelt advised: Every year, do something new – learn something, create something, do something that will keep you fresh and growing. A bucket list can be helpful. In 2003, my daughter Heather gave me *A Walk in The Woods* by Bill Bryson, a one-of-a-kind and wonderful book. Since that time, I've wanted to hike the Appalachian Trail. In 2022, I accomplished this goal in a scaled-down way with Alan Baker, Krishna Bhatta, Mark Brooks, Kaveh Haghkerdar, Robert Strong, Walter Ulmer, and Pete Vigue at Rainbow Lake in the Maine north woods. Admittedly, our hike was short, but we loved it. I have two items to go: I would like to teach at sea. I've always wanted to do this since attending fascinating lectures on The Queen Elizabeth on the way to Europe in 1963. I would also like to teach in Asia. I've had the opportunity to do this in the past, but commitments didn't allow the time required. My bucket list isn't critical to do, but I sure would enjoy these new adventures.

If you are asked to teach a course on Organizational Consulting, see the syllabus in Appendix B. It works well but will work best if you prepare stories and anecdotes from your personal experience. Nothing beats lessons learned first hand and the discussion that results. This book concludes with advice for consulting success and a timeless truth. The advice comes from legendary coach John Wooden's father who said, "Show up and do your best, be kind and help others, and make your life your masterpiece." The timeless truth is, "You can't please everyone. You're not a pizza." My best wishes, George Manning

Appendix A

Books

The following are books I use in my consulting practice (some are classics, some are new, all are helpful):

Psychology textbooks include personality, abnormal, developmental, biological, health, counseling, behavioral, perception, social, cognition, motivation, learning, and industrial.

Topical books include:

- **A.** *A Business and its Beliefs* by Thomas J. Watson; *A Class Divided* by Jane Elliott; *A Great Place to Work* by Robert Levering; *A Little History of the World* by E.H. Gombrich; *Albion's Seed* by David Hatchett Fischer; *Anatomy of an Illness* by Norman Cousins; *An American Journey* by Colin Powell; *Authentic Leadership* by Bill George.

- **B.** *Behave* by Robert Sapolsky; *Built to Last* by James Collins; *Benjamin Franklin* by Walter Isaacson.

- **C.** *Cognitive Behavior Therapy* by Albert Ellis; *Coping with Difficult People* by Robert Bramson; *Crucial Conversations* by Joseph Grenny and Kerry Patterson; *Crucibles of Leadership* by Warren Bennis.

- **D.** *Deep Work* by Cal Newport; *Democracy and Education* by John Dewey; *Drive* by Daniel Pink.

- **E.** *Economics* by Paul Samuelson; *Eight Habits of the Heart* by Clifton Taulbert; *Emerson's Essays* by Ralph Waldo Emerson; *Emotional Intelligence* by Daniel Goleman; *Evicted* by Matthew Desmond; *Execution* by Larry Bossidy; *Executive* by Harry Levinson.

- **F.** *First Things First* by Stephen R. Covey; *First, Break All the Rules* by Marcus Buckingham; *Flow* by Mihaly Csikszentmihalyi; *Folkways* by William Graham Sumner; *Fraternity* by Diane Brady; *Full Range Leadership* by Bruce Avolio; *Future Shock* by Alvin Toffler; *FYI – For Your Improvement* by Heather Barnfield and Michael Lombardo.

- **G.** *Gift from the Sea* by Anne Morrow Lindbergh; *Good to Great* by James Collins; *Groupthink* by Irving Janis; *Growth Psychology* by Duane Schultz.

- **H.** *Handbooks of Structured Experience* by William Pfeiffer and John Jones; *Hardwiring Excellence* by Quint Studer; *Harry Truman's Excellent Adventure* by Matthew Algeo; *Hillbilly Elegy* by J.D. Vance; *How Doctors Think* by Jerome Groopman; *How Starbucks Saved My Life* by Michael Gill; *How the Irish Saved Civilization* by Thomas Cahill; *How the Mighty Fall* by James Collins; *How to Win Friends and*

Influence People by Dale Carnegie; *How We Die* by Sherwin Nuland; *Human Behavior* by Bernard Berelson and Gary Steiner.

- **I.** *If Aristotle Ran General Motors* by Tom Morris; *If You Meet the Buddha on the Road, Kill Him!* by Sheldon Kopp; *In Search of Excellence* by Tom Peters and Bob Waterman; *Intellectuals* by Paul Johnson; *In the Heart of the Sea* by Nathaniel Philbrick; *Influence* by Robert Cialdini; *Integrating the Individual and the Organization* by Chris Argyris; *Introduction to Psychoanalysis* by Sigmund Freud; *Is It Worth Dying For?* by Robert S. Eliot; *It's The Manager* by Jim Clifton; *It's Your Ship* by Michael Abrashoff.

- **J.** *Jesus CEO* by Laurie Beth Jones.

- **K.** *Killer Angels* by Michael Shaara; *Kurt Hahn's Schools and Legacy* by Martin Flavin.

- **L.** *Leaders Eat Last* by Simon Sinek; *Leadership* by James Macgregor Burns; *Leadership Without Easy Answers* by Ronald Heifetz; *Leading Change* by John Kotter; *Lean In* by Sheryl Sandberg; *Learned Optimism* by Martin Seligman; *Lincoln* by Herbert Donald; *Lives in Progress* by Robert White; *Living, Loving, and Learning* by Leo Buscaglio; *Love and Profit* by James Autry; *Love and Will* by Rollo May.

- **M.** *Maid* by Stephanie Land; *Make Your Bed* by William McRaven; *Man Against Himself* by Karl Menninger; *Management by Objectives* by George Odiorne; *Man's Search for Meaning* by Viktor Frankl; *Modern Man in Search of a Soul* by Carl Jung; *Motivation and Personality* by Abraham

Maslow; *Motivation and Productivity* by Saul Gellerman; *Multiple Intelligences* by Howard Gardner.

- **N.** *Neurosis and Human Growth* by Karen Horney; *New Patterns of Management* by Rensis Likert; *Nickel and Dimed* by Barbara Ehrenreich; *Night* by Elie Wiesel; *Nothing but the Truth* by Avi; *Now, Discover Your Strengths* by Marcus Buckingham; *Nuts!* by Kevin and Jackie Freiberg.

- **O.** *Organizational Culture and Leadership* by Edgar Schein; *On Becoming a Leader* by Warren Bennis; *On Becoming a Person* by Carl Rogers; *On Death and Dying* by Elizabeth Kubler Ross; *On Leadership* by John Gardner; *On Liberty* by John Stuart Mill; *On Writing* by Stephen King; *Open Book Management* by John Case; *Out of The Crisis* by W. Edwards Deming.

- **P.** *Paradigm Shift* by Joel Barker; *Plato, Not Prozac* by Lou Marinoff; *Productive Workplaces* by Marvin Weisbord; *Psychology and Work Today* by Duane Schultz.

- **Q.** *Quiet* by Susan Cain.

- **R.** *Rational Emotive Behavior Therapy* by Albert Ellis.

- **S.** *Sabbath* by Wayne Muller; *Sailing the Wine-Dark Sea* by Thomas Cahill; *Sapiens* by Yuval Noah Harari; *Season of Life* by Jeffrey Marx; *Self-Efficacy* by Albert Bandura; *Servant Leadership* by Robert Greenleaf; *Shackleton's Way* by Margot Morrell; *Siddartha* by Herman Hesse; *Social Intelligence* by Daniel Goleman; *Soul Pancake* by Rainn Wilson; *Stress Without Distress* by Hans Selye.

- **T.** *Team of Rivals* by Doris Kearns Goodwin; *Ten Commandments for Business Failure* by Donald Keough; *The 21 Irrefutable Laws of Leadership* by John Maxwell; *The 7 Habits of Highly Effective People* by Stephen Covey; *The Achievement Motive* by David McClelland; *The Advantage* by Patrick Lencioni; *The Adventures of Tom Sawyer* by Mark Twain; *The Art of Loving* by Erich Fromm; *The Bass Handbook of Leadership* by Bernard Bass; *The Bible* (Old and New Testament), *The Blank Slate* by Steven Pinker; *The Body Keeps the Score* by Bessel van der Kolk; *The Cave and the Light* by Arthur Herrman; *The Checklist Manifesto* by Atul Gawande; *The Choice* by Edith Eva Eger; *The Coming Job Wars* by Jim Clifton; *The Defining Decade* by Meg Jay; *The Dream Manager* by Matthew Kelly; *The Effective Executive* by Peter Drucker; *The Erik Erikson Reader* by Robert Coles; *The Essential Drucker* by Peter Drucker; *The Five Dysfunctions of a Team* by Patrick Lencioni; *The Gene* by Siddartha Mukherjee; *The Greatest Generation* by Tom Brokaw; *The Greatest Salesman in the World* by Og Mandino; *The Happiness Project* by Gretchen Rubin; *The Hard Hat* by Jon Gordon; *The Human Equation* by Jeffrey Pfeffer; *The Human Side of Enterprise* by Douglas McGregor; *The Human Touch* by William Arnold and Jeanne Plas; *The Idea Factory* by Jon Gertner; *The Iliad and the Odyssey* by Homer; *The Innovators* by Walter Isaacson; *The Last Lecture* by Randy Pausch; *The Leader's Bookshelf* by James Stavridis; *The Leader's Companion* by J. Thomas Wren; *The Leadership Challenge* by James Kouzes and Barry Posner; *The Life of Pi* by Yann Martel; *The Little Prince* by Antoine de Saint-Exupery; *The Lobster Coast* by Colin Woodard; *The Multipliers* by Liz Wiseman; *The Myth of Sisyphus* by Albert Camus; *The Naked Ape* by Desmond Morris; *The Nature of Human*

Intelligence by Robert Sternberg; *The Nature of Managerial Work* by Henry Mintzberg; *The Nature of Prejudice* by Gordon Allport; *The One Minute Manager* by Ken Blanchard; *The People Puzzle* by Morris Massey; *The People's House* by David Pepper; *The Practice of Management* by Peter Drucker; *The Principles of Psychology* by William James; *The Power of Positive Thinking* by Norman Vincent Peale; *The Principles of Scientific Management* by Frederick Taylor; *The Prophet* by Kahlil Gibran; *The Reckoning* by David Halberstam; *The Republic* by Plato; *The Richest Man in Babylon* by George Clason; *The Rhinoceros* by Eugene Ionesco; *The Righteous Mind* by Jonathan Haidt; *The Road Less Traveled* by Scott Peck; *The Screwtape Letters* by C. S. Lewis; *The Servant* by James Hunter; *The Storm of War* by Andrew Roberts; *The Stress of Life* by Hans Selye; *The Toyota Way* by Jeffrey Liker; *The Traveler's Gift* by Andy Andrews; *The Warmth of Other Suns* by Isabel Wilkerson; *The Wealth of Nations* by Adam Smith; *The Wisdom of The Body* by Walter Cannon; *The Worldly Philosophers* by Robert Heilbroner; *Theodore Rex* by Edmund Morris; *Theories of Personality* by Duane Schultz; *Think and Grow Rich* by Napoleon Hill; *Touch the Top of the World* by Erik Weihenmayer; *Toward a Psychology of Being* by Abraham Maslow; *Toyota Culture* by Jeffrey Liker; *Transitions* by William Bridges; *True North* by Bill George; *Turn the Ship Around!* by David Marquet; *Type A Behavior and Your Heart* by Meyer Friedman.

- **U.** *Uncle Tom's Cabin* by Harriet Beecher Stowe; *Uncommon Friends* by James Newton; *Understanding Human Nature* by Alfred Adler; *Up the Organization* by Robert Townsend.

- **V.** *Values Shift* by Lynn Paine.

Lifetime Lessons in Consulting 215

- **W.** *What Got You Here Won't Get You There* by Marshall Goldsmith; *What Color is Your Parachute?* by Richard Bolles; *Walden* by Henry David Thoreau; *Walden Two* by B. F. Skinner; *Walk in My Combat Boots* by James Patterson; *Washington: A Life* by Ron Chernow; *Who Says Elephants Can't Dance?* by Louis Gerstner; *Why Zebras Don't Get Ulcers* by Robert Sapolsky; *Winning* by Jack Welch; *Winston Churchill* by Andrew Roberts; *Wooden on Leadership* by John Wooden; *Work Motivation in Organizational Behavior* by Craig Pinder; *Work Rules!* by Laszlo Bock; *Working* by Studs Terkel.

Reference books include: *The Merriam-Webster Dictionary*, *The Encyclopedia Britannica*, and *Oxford's Atlas of The World*.

Fiction books stimulate your mind, enrich your life, and make you more interesting. Examples range from *Don Quixote* to *Uncle Tom's Cabin*.

Appendix B

Syllabus

The following is the syllabus I use for Organizational Consulting:

PSY 645 Organizational Consulting
Instructor: George Manning
Location: Business, Education, Psychology Building

Course description: This course presents a comprehensive overview of organizational consulting, including its history, specializations and contexts. Fundamental principles, effective practices, and emerging issues will be studied. The "mindset" of the contemporary consultant will be the focus of the course with special attention to education, skills and professional integrity. Students will read and discuss a text on the contemporary consulting industry and a reader on consulting as a professional calling. The course includes panel presentations and insights from practitioners, gate keepers and buyers of consulting services. Students will complete a term project that will personalize learning.

Course Resources:
- Text – *The Contemporary Consultant: Handbook of Management Consulting*, Larry Greiner and Flemming Poulfelt (eds.), Thomson South-Western, U.S., 2005. This text provides a comprehensive overview of the current status of the consulting industry. It is written by world experts who provide information and insight. Historical perspectives and practical examples assure a useful text for academics, practitioners and users of consulting services. Contents include 1) consulting skills and professionalism, 2) major practice areas in consulting (IT, strategy and organization, marketing, operations, and human resource consulting), 3) consulting in different contexts (CEO and Boards, global consulting, and public sector consulting), 4) intervention and solution strategies, 5) managing and growing a consulting firm, and 6) the future of organizational consulting.
- Reader – *The Consultant's Calling: Bringing Who You Are to What You Do*, Goeffrey M. Bellman, Jossey-Bass, San Francisco, 2002. This book provides a portrayal of consulting as a way of life rather than an abstract function. It will be of interest to anyone who wants to know what consulting is as a career, as a living, as a life. Contents include foundations for the work, building client relationships, the proper use of influence, understanding organizations, succeeding in the market place, and the quest for meaning through work.
- Handouts – provided as needed
- Related books include – *Consulting Success* by Michael Zipursky; *Flawless Consulting* by Peter Block; *Humanistic Consulting* by David Noer; *The Consulting Bible* by Alan Weiss; *The Consultant's Handbook* by Samir Parikh; *The McKinsey Way* by Ethan Rasiel; and *The Mind of a Consultant* by Sandeep Krishman

Student Learning Outcomes:
1. Knowledge of the contemporary consulting industry, including contexts and practice areas.
2. Knowledge of the consulting profession as a way of life, including challenges, satisfactions and current issues.

Methods of Assessing Student Learning:
1. Participation – Students are expected to be proactive learners. This includes attendance at all classes and active participation in discussion and class activities.
2. Course journal (one to two page reaction entry on each Part of the text (6), each half of the reader (2), and each class panel/presentation (10), including: 1) related personal experience; 2) personal beliefs and opinions; 3) issues and questions triggered; 4) what was interesting or useful that you want to remember). Evaluation will be based on knowledge, comprehension and application of the subject.
3. Term project (approximately 20 pages with minimum of 10 references; no more than three Internet references with no .com). Options include case study/experience report; term paper on consulting topic of interest; feasibility paper or written plan to be a consultant (APA style/format). Assessment will be based on analysis, synthesis and evaluation of literature on the subject.

Session I Friday, May 15 6:15 – 9:00 p.m.
- Introductions
- Preview of course and learning outcomes: This is a comprehensive course about the field of organizational consulting – history, current practice areas, and future challenges. It is also a course about being a consultant and doing the work, including the preparation, attitude, skills and principles

of successful consulting. Students will learn the products, processes, problems, principles and practices of organizational consulting.
- The professor's lens – stories, anecdotes, and lessons learned

Guest presentations and discussions:

Who? Ron Heineman, CEO, ELS Human Resource Solutions
Topic: Human Resource Outsourcing and Executive Coaching
Questions: What do you do? How do you do it? What are the results? What are the issues and trends in HR outsourcing?

Who? Jennifer Graft/Doug Mathews/Terri Logan, Right Management Consulting
Topic: Products and Services of a National Firm, including outplacement consulting and assessment
Questions: What is the nature of your work? Who uses your services? What is the history, current status, and likely future for outplacement consulting and executive services?

Who? Peter Jordan, Vice President, Radisson Hotels; Bob Herrick, The Health Alliance
Topic(s): Hospitality Consulting; Healthcare Consulting; Performance Improvement
Questions: What is the nature of your work? What are the costs and benefits of performance improvement consulting?

Who? Terri Stewart, Just the Basics; Linda Gravett, Gravett Consulting Associates; Rebecca White, Director, Fifth Third Entrepreneurship Institute
Topic(s): The Entrepreneurship Spirit; Starting and Sustaining a Consulting Practice; Non-profit/Social Agency Consulting
Questions: What are the ingredients of a successful consulting practice, firm, company? What are 5 musts for business success with case(s) in point?

- Observations, questions and open discussion (including SALTS)
- Homework assignment – Text Part 1, The Consulting Industry, Skills and Professionalism; Text Part 2, Major Practicing Areas in Consulting (IT, strategy and organization, marketing, operations, human resource consulting)

Sessions II and III Saturday, May 16 9:00 a.m. – 5:00 p.m.
- Text chapters and discussion – Text Part 1, The Consulting Industry, Skills and Professionalism; Text Part 2, Major Practicing Areas in Consulting (IT, strategy and organization, marketing, operations, human resource consulting)
- Term project progress report
- Guest presentations and discussion
    Who? Peter Block, author and consultant; Connie Burkart, Vice President, Human Resource Development, Western Southern Insurance Company; Gordon Duke, Duke and Associates, former Secretary of Finance, Commonwealth of Kentucky; Patti Holmes, Holmes Associates; Evan Gay, organizational consultant; Grant Karnes, CM/PG Cost Management Performance Group; Steve Martin, Vice President, Organization Development, The

Huber Company; Diane Strickland-Jordan, Managing Principal, HRC Consulting Group; Amy Stoll, Director of Organizational Effectiveness, Cincinnati Children's Hospital Medical Center; Rob Snyder, Executive Director, METS, Northern Kentucky University; John Wagner, Vice President, Labor Relations, The Kroger Company; Vince Brown, President, Global Lead; John Rees, COO, Corrections Corporation of America/Secretary of Corrections, Commonwealth of Kentucky; Jeff Groob, Groob and Associates.

Topic(s):
1. University sponsored consulting services
2. Getting Started as an Organizational Consultant (including trials, tribulations and triumphs)
3. Growing and Maintaining a Consulting Practice (including a day in the life of a consultant)
4. Management, Financial and IT Consulting (including business, government and not-for-profit perspectives)
5. Industrial/Organizational Consulting (including Personnel Assessment and Management Development)
6. Products and Services of a Local Firm (including compensation consulting)
7. Cost Management and Performance Consulting (including expense reduction, performance improvement, and organization design)
8. Special Challenges of Diversity, Political, Healthcare, Criminal Justice, and Labor Relations Consulting

Questions: What do you do? How do you do it? What are the results? What are the satisfactions and frustrations?

What are the issues and trends in your field of consulting? What are the best practices being used?

- Tutorial – Building Community in the Workplace (interventions and cases)
- Observations, questions and open discussion (including SALTS)
- Homework assignment – Text Part 3, Consulting in Different Contexts; Text Part 4, Implementation and Change; Text Part 5, Managing and Growing the Consulting Firm; Reader – *The Consultant's Calling*, 1st half of book

Session IV Friday, June 12 6:15 – 9:00 p.m.
- Text chapter and discussion – Text Part 3, Consulting in Different Contexts (CEO and boards, global consulting, and public sector consulting)
- Term project progress report
- Guest presentations and discussion

    Who? Tom Hayes, Legal and Business Consultant; Wendy Nepute, Director of Organizational Consulting, Cincinnati Children's Hospital Medical Center; Joan Fox, Fox Consulting Associates; Mark Donaghey, General Manager of Dayton (RTA).

    Topic(s):
    1. What consulting services do businesses really need? Observations of a CEO turned consultant
    2. Challenges and satisfactions of internal consulting in a large organization
    3. Challenges and Satisfactions of external consulting, including physical and social demands of travel
    4. Issues and trends in business, transportation, healthcare, and customer service consulting

Questions: What do you do? How do you do it? What are the results? What are the qualities of a successful internal/external consultant? What are the do's and don'ts of marketing oneself as a consultant?

- Observations, questions and open discussion (including SALTS)

Sessions V and VI Saturday, June 13 9:00 a.m. – 5:00 p.m.
- Reader – *The Consultant's Calling*, 1st half of book
- Term project progress report
- Guest presentations and discussion

    Who? Bob Veverka, Executive Director, Executive Education, College of Business, University of Cincinnati; Gerry Kaminski, Organizational Improvement, Cincinnati Children's Hospital; Nancy Byrd, Vice President, Human Resources Development, The Health Alliance; Dan Keefe, Vice President, Human Resources, Great American Insurance Company; Paul Quealy, Vice President, Human Resources, Milacron; Gema Bahns, Director, Hispanic Business Development, Fifth Third Bank; Jenny Skinner, Vice President, Organization Development, Tri Health; Mary Martin, Vice President, Education and Development, Federated Department Stores; Gordon Barnhart, President, The Compass Group; Henry Cohen, Cohen and Associates; Dick Boyle, former president of Kentucky Power/Vice President of Commercial Operations, American Electric Power; David Hrovat, Director of International Studies/Development, Northern Kentucky University.

    Topic(s):
    1. Organizational Consulting Do's and Don'ts – Secrets to Success and Biggest Mistakes

2. Psychological Consulting Services
3. Managing External Consultants
4. International Consulting – special challenges
5. Issues and trends in university/institute sponsored consulting services
6. Using the internet for marketing consulting services

Questions? Gatekeeping and standards—who hires and coordinates external/internal consultants? What are your experiences, policies and practices? What qualities do you seek in an organizational consultant? What problems do you encounter?

- Tutorial – Fostering a High Performance Workplace (interventions and cases)
- Observations, questions and open discussion (including SALTS)
- Homework assignment – Reader, *The Consultant's Calling*, second half of book

Session VII Friday, July 17 6:15 – 9:00 p.m.
- Guest presentations and discussion
    Who? Greg Love, Director of Coaching and Development, 5/3rd Bank; Steve McMillen, former Chief Learning Officer, Thomson Publishing, Hillenbrand Industries, O'Charley's, Inc.; Dale Browning, CEO Tech Collaboration; Mike Ellis, Independent Consultant, Northern Kentucky University.

    Topic:
    1. Executive leadership/coaching
    2. Large scale technical consulting

3. Preparation and training for a consulting career
   4. Time, money, people – activity/discussion

   Questions: What are typical career paths for organizational consultants? What are the satisfactions and frustrations of being a consultant in small, middle, and large organizations?

- Observations, questions and open discussion (including SALTS)

Sessions VIII and IX Saturday, July 18 9:00 a.m. – 5:00 p.m.
- Text chapter and discussion – Text Part 4, Implementation and Change; Text Part 5, Managing and Growing the Consulting Firm
- Term project progress report
- Guest presentations and discussion
  Who? Gail Love, Love Associates; Bob Edwards, Edwards Management Consultants; Michael Washington, Professor, Northern Kentucky University; Beverly Watts, Watts Associates/former Director, Kentucky Commission on Human Rights; Maria White, Consultant Partner, Pope and Associates; Sue Russell, Russell Associates; Chai Voris, President, Dynamic Change Solutions; David Krings, Krings Associates/former President of International Association of City and County Administrators; Michael O'Brien, O'Brien Group; George Stoll, Stoll Associates; Diane Menendez, Executive Development, Fifth Third Bank; Margaret Casarez, Executive Director, The Phoenix Place; Phil Jones, Director, Xavier Consulting Institute, Xavier University.

Topics:
1. Diversity Consulting in American Business, Industry and Government
2. Managing Organizational Change (including personal experience and lessons learned)
3. Principles, Practices and Examples of Public sector consulting
4. Quality Improvement Consulting (current themes and practices)
5. Consulting Relationships – What Works/What Doesn't Work?
6. Community social change consulting
7. Finding your nich (calling)

Questions: What are the forms of consulting partnerships? What are the principles and practices that should be followed? What are the customs and best practices for being paid for consulting services?

- Tutorial – Helping People Through Change (interventions and cases)
- Observations, questions and open discussion (including SALTS)
- Homework assignment – Text Part 5, Managing and Growing the Consulting Firm; Text Part 6, Looking Ahead at Management Consulting; and Reader – *The Consultant's Calling*, second half of book

Session X Friday, August 14 6:15 – 8:00 p.m.
- Text chapter and discussion – Text Part 6, Looking Ahead at Management Consulting; Reader – *The Consultant's Calling*, second half of book
- Term project progress report

- Guest Presentations and Discussion
    Who? Jeff Walter, Vice President, Human Resource Development, Great American Insurance Company; Mike Campbell, Director (ret), Kentucky Power Company
    Topic(s): Organizational Consulting – The Role and Challenges of Internal/External Consultants; The Life of a consultant – Capstone questions and answers
    Questions: What do you do? How do you do it? What are the satisfactions and frustrations of consulting? What are the issues and trends in organizational consulting? What are the personal and professional pitfalls to avoid in providing consulting services?

    Who? Matt Shank, Dean of Business, University of Dayton
    Topic: Marketing Consulting/Marketing Consulting Services

- Observations, questions, and open discussion (including SALTS)

Sessions XI and XII Saturday, August 15 9:00a.m. – 5:00 p.m.
   Who? Organization Owner/Presidents (Young Presidents Organization (YPO/SPO) panel –Larry Albice, Jim Akers, Bert Amann, Wick Auk, Jim Bushman, Wayne Carlisle, Jack Cook, Bob Coughlin, Mark Daly, Allen Dohan, Tom Frinkman, Thomas Gerdes, Bob Johnson, Steve Kent, Shenan Murphy, Chip Nielson, Jim Pearce, Rene Robichard, Kevin Roche, Jane Rollinson, Rob Sibcy, Bob Scanlon, Gary Thompson, Marius Van Melle, Bill Ward, Claus von Zychlin).
   Topic: Using Organizational Consultants

Questions? Who do you hire to do what and why? How do you find them, pick them, and pay them? Success stories, mistakes made, and lessons learned.

- Observations, questions and open discussion (including SALTS)
- Course Journal due and discussion
- Term project due and discussion
- Tutorial – Group Dynamics and Processes (interventions and cases)
- Course review and evaluation

TERM PROJECT EXAMPLES

Case study/experience Report

Example

IRS service improvement and reorganization initiative – who, what, why, when, where, how report including results and lessons learned.

Term Paper on Consulting Topic

Examples
1. Building client relationship
2. The use of influence
3. Organization success factors
4. Succeeding in the market place
5. The quest for meaning

Feasibility Plan To Be A Consultant

Examples
1. IT
2. Strategy and Organization
3. Marketing
4. Operations
5. Human resources

Appendix C

Lessons Learned

The following are personal and professional lessons I've learned over 52 years of consulting:

#1 – Having fundamental knowledge about a subject is important to being a successful consultant. It's important to stay current in one's field.

#2 – Visit foreign places, be personally humble, make good friends.

#3 – Get the facts before making a decision. Be true to yourself and you can't be false to others. When you are doing the wrong thing, stop; when you are in the wrong place, leave.

#4 – Finding one's niche or calling is fundamental to a satisfying and productive life for every person.

#5 – A broken heart can hurt as much as a broken leg. Hearts heal quickly and aches are temporary when people are young, so don't do anything foolish.

#6 – Prepare for business meetings. Three questions must be answered with a 'yes' for a job to be right: Can you do the job at the level of deliverable required? Do you want to do the job? Is there a good psycho-social fit?

#7 – Graduation isn't just for graduates; it's also for those who care about them and want to celebrate their success.
    – The three most important questions facing a young person are 1. Who are you? 2. What do you want to do? Who do you want to be with? Problems come when one addresses these questions out of order.

#8 – The three secrets to happiness are: 1. having someone to love; 2. having something important to do; 3. counting one's blessings.

#9 – Second chances are good if one takes responsibility, learns from mistakes, has a positive attitude, and works hard.

#10– Say yes to challenges. Just because you haven't done something doesn't mean you can't learn to do it.
    – Emergencies happen, and clients have mission-critical events that consultants must honor and help address.

#11 – We are like crayons in a box – some are bright and shiny, some are soft and warm; some are used a lot, some are new and pointy; Together, we make a beautiful world. In any case, we all have to live in the same box.

#12 – Follow five consulting principles: 1. Always focus on mission and values versus style and technique (putting client interest first). 2. Always tell the truth as you see it (with kindness). 3. Always keep job knowledge current (concepts and skills). 4. Always plan and

prepare thoroughly but remain flexible (whatever it takes). and 5. Always deliver superior results (satisfaction guaranteed).

– Personal honesty, knowing your subject, working hard, and caring about your client are the essential ingredients of consulting success.

– In moral dilemmas, use your best thinking, listen to your heart, and let reason be your guide. Never knowingly do harm to others; and when in doubt, always do the loving thing.

#13 – Care about the client, ask questions that require client thought, listen carefully versus talking, champion principle-based actions to solve problems and advance the organization.

#14 – Most successful leaders genuinely care about young people and their development.

#15 – No two people are exactly alike in their interests and temperaments, even if they share the same goals; keep your eyes wide open before marriage and half shut afterward; the two best things in the world are the infinity of the universe and the intimacy of a close relationship.

#16 – Our lives are determined by what we think about ourselves, the people we are around, and the books we read.

#17 – Successful consulting requires listening to the client, keeping an open mind, focusing on the client's important and timely needs, and the ability to change gears and direction quickly.

– Good outcomes begin and end with good relationships and these are based on mutual respect and trust built over time.

– There is usually more caught than taught, and most people go by the behaviors they see more than by the words they hear. Valuing diversity is shown through mutual respect, trust, and support.

— Consulting success requires establishing productive relationships based on trust and shared commitments.

— The consultant who is intellectually and personally honest won't do something she thinks is wrong and will always do what she thinks is right.

— The successful consultant is humble, has a sense of humor, and is focused on meeting client needs.

#18 — A consultant must live by the highest standards of moral conduct. This is especially true in two areas — human relations and financial matters.

#19 — Labor and management leaders can take the low road of a power struggle that can destroy a company or take the high road of working together to create lasting success. Which path is taken depends on the goodwill and practices of leaders on both sides of the table. Labor and management agreement on core values and supporting actions is the strength of an organization.

— It is important to involve people in matters that affect them.

— The physical energy, enthusiasm, competence, and commitment of leaders can stimulate the performance of government personnel to a level fully as great as the private sector. It is important to know your customer and be able to keep secrets till the timing is right.

— Expect the unexpected and truth is stranger than fiction.

— When you spend a night in a nursing home, you soon become staff and learn firsthand how important, satisfying, and *demanding* this meaningful work is. There are many people who work in caregiving positions, who deserve the deepest respect and greatest appreciation society can give.

#20 — A caring and committed leader can assemble a team and achieve enormous success by having clear goals and creating a positive work culture . . . including government.

— Spend time when a study or action group first forms to agree upon goals and norms of behavior.

— Honest, thoughtful, and decisive leadership works well across cultures; collaboration across work units and disciplines boosts morale; when leaders model and support goodwill, performance rises to extraordinary levels.

— Leaders can be obstacles to creating a positive work climate, or if they are the kind of people who want a healthy work culture, they can usually have it. They may have to work hard for it, and it will take time and resources, but if leaders want to achieve a positive and healthy human environment, it can be done under almost any circumstances.

— It's important to have the active and well-conceived involvement of leaders developing leaders in a company. Otherwise, time, attention, and resources are poorly spent.

— The senior leaders of an organization must have mutual respect, interpersonal trust, and a one-team attitude with each other as an example for others.

— When leading change, have a good reason for making change, involve the people who will be impacted by change, go slow enough so people can adjust, keep people informed through unambiguous and constant communication, provide training in new knowledge and skill to support change, wait patiently for results, acknowledge and reward people for adapting to change.

— When leaders and front-line personnel have a shared goal and work together cooperatively to achieve it, the result can be magnificent.

#21 – Using time management principles can help one be twice as productive and half as stressed as one would be without this job aid for life and work.

#22 – Most international owners (German, French, Italian, English, Japanese, Swedish, American, etc.) value the perspectives

and talents of different cultures, but the ultimate and final decision-making is the responsibility of owners.

– The most effective leaders have an integrative approach. They integrate diverse cultures, races, genders, and personalities into a whole that is greater than the sum of its parts. The integration is not a melting-down process; rather, it's a building up in which the identity of the individual is preserved yet simultaneously transcended.

#23 – It's essential to work with the client to be sure the consulting content and delivery are tailored to the needs of the audience.

– Adjusting to change is challenging. Leaders can make the difference between positive and negative outcomes by modeling and reinforcing effective coping skills.

– Good companies hunger for ways to keep their employees well-trained.

– Senior leaders must understand and visibly support consulting initiatives for maximum success; the consultant must have believability and passion for the subject.

– Human resource initiatives work well when they fit the organization's culture and priority needs.

– Effective management is necessary for company success; education can help keep managers stimulated and growing throughout their careers.

#24 – The time and skill needed to create good media is enormous ... but worth it. Working with talented people sharing a common cause is highly enjoyable.

#25 – There are three markers of a good retirement: physical fitness, social connectedness, and sufficient income. There are two inoculators against a bad retirement: someone to love and something important to do. There is a one-sentence recipe for a suc-

cessful retirement: Move your body, open your mind, follow your heart, and count your blessings.

– Every day do something for your physical, social, spiritual, and occupational wellbeing, and view life as a marathon, not a sprint. The happiest people don't have the best of everything, they make the best of everything they have.

– If leaders don't understand, appreciate, and support employees, stress levels go up. If they don't perform their own work well, causing extra stress for others, stress goes higher. If they don't do their own work right and things go wrong and they blame it on others, they are stress carriers.

– Leaders must keep standards of behavior high, including zero tolerance for bullying and inappropriate sexual language or conduct.

#26 – In the workplace, keep reporting and love relationships separate; ladies and gentlemen must treat each other as such.

#27 – Site visits, interviews, and observations help prepare the consultant by providing important information and context.

#28 – Dress appropriately to communicate respect and professionalism and be prepared for emergencies by keeping business clothes with you.

– There are some things you can't change, such as your voice and other physical features. In consulting, these are over-shadowed by content and character.

#29 – Great consultants guide and facilitate – not command and control.

#30 – The successful consultant must be a continuous learner; every teacher needs a teacher.

– 1. Focus on others, put their interests first; 2. Be a team player, teach others the rides; 3. Be professional in conduct and try your best.

#31 – Clients appreciate a simple and logical approach to planning, executing, and evaluating consulting services. They think it's professional and gives them peace of mind to evaluate pace, relevance, value, and participation.

#32 – There is a saying – *early to bed, early to rise, work hard and advertise*. The best advertisement is word of mouth testimony and a good story.

#33 – You don't have to attend every argument you are invited to. Make war on your vices, keep peace in the family, do good work with dear friends.

#34 – When unexpected things happen, don't panic. Think about cause and effect and study the situation.
– Outdoor learning initiatives must be safe above all. With guided discussion, they can help build positive relationships and effective teamwork in the workplace.

#35 – Funding for consulting services can be creative, including consulting for trade and third-party payment.

#36 – There may be a time in your career when preparation is easy, but most of the time you will be working hard to learn, or you will be working equally hard to remember so that your work is always well done.

#37 – Learn as if you were going to live forever. A core characteristic of an effective consultant is the love of learning.

#38 – Medical emergencies can happen to anyone, at any time, and any place. If medical conditions can be worked around, do so. If it's humanly possible to meet client needs, the consultant must deliver. This is appreciated and the reward is mutual loyalty.

#39 – Fatigue is real – the inability to do more work because of previous work. One must rest well to work well.

#40 – Positive self-talk, family and friends, and good books help us live full and meaningful lives.
  – A book read at the right time can change everything that follows. Ideas, truths, principles, metaphors, and exercises in books can help meet the needs and circumstances of the client.

#41 – The client who hires you may not be present to pay you and neither an agreement letter nor a signed contract is a guarantee of payment. If it's a molehill, don't make it a mountain – let it go.
  – Do what you love, for the right reasons, in the right way, and *enough* money will follow. Never charge more than you would be willing to pay.

#42 – Save time, solve problems, and build goodwill by keeping good records of consulting services, including financial information.

#43 – A company must manage its consultants or consultants will manage the company. Consultants may be expert and well-meaning, but clients must stay intentionally involved to manage their services for the best results. A clearly understood client-consultant compact is indispensable.

#44 – Good people make good leaders and good employees, and together they make great companies.

— Good health is critical for successful consulting and a key is to have a primary care physician who knows you well.

— If you are addressing a group, protect your voice and drink lots of water.

#45 — Being mindful is not only a spiritual concept, but also a practical principle for safe behavior.

— Always keep a notepad and pencil with you wherever you are — bedstand, bathroom, kitchen, and car. You never know when you will have a thought or idea that must be captured.

#46 — Home is the universal haven of the odd, dissenting and free ... where they have to take you in.

#47 — No turtle ever got on a fencepost by itself.

#48 — Celebrate the common goodness in all people and the special perspectives and talents of diverse people.

#49 — Both teaching and consulting are other-serving activities. If you are truly learner-centered, you will be a successful professor. If you are truly client-focused, you will be a successful consultant.

#50 — Clients expect consultants to be aware of current information and empirical data. The Gallup organization is a trusted partner in providing accurate and useful survey information.

#51 — One must keep up with changes in the cyber world to be an effective consultant. This includes proficiency in the use of computers and phones.

— The successful consultant must be eternal in principle and agile in delivery.

#52 – Presentations on the theory and practice of leadership are most popular and helpful when a qualified person provides the theory and a highly respected leader in the field shares personal experience, practical application, and useful advice to the audience. It's especially helpful when leaders share mistakes they have made and what they learned from them.

#53 – Involve the client for lasting impact. Client understanding, ownership, and effectiveness increase in proportion to personal involvement.

#54 – The successful consultant is a super teabag with a can-do spirit and a 'whatever it takes' attitude. The client hopes the consultant will plan and prepare thoroughly and will not make preventable mistakes of either omission or commission; and will handle unpreventable problems and emergencies calmly and intelligently. A saying that originated in England during World War II gives good guidance – keep calm and carry on. Do this, and clients will love it.

#55 – The best advertising is word-of-mouth recommendations from respected people. This is especially the case when consulting services impact a client's health, wealth, and reputation. Consulting is based on trusting relationships that are built over time – client by client, service by service.

#56 – Every person has a unique personality that is not likely to change. Consulting success requires flexibility to understand, appreciate, and deal effectively with a wide variety of people.

#57 – Caring about the work and caring about people are the two essential requirements for effective leadership. Good leaders also have integrity, job knowledge, and people-building skills.

#58 – 1. Write what you know about; 2. Write the way you talk; 3. Write, read, and re-write for clarity; 4. Proof for errors, including spelling; 5. Write logically. You are meant to write if time stands still when you do.

#59 – Leaders from private businesses, government agencies, and non-profit organizations admire each other and enjoy working together on projects of common interest. Learning, working, and serving together is satisfying and results in meaningful accomplishments.

#60 – Have an exit philosophy for your life and work. Don't let the old man in.

#61 – Take your work seriously, but don't exaggerate your importance. A little humility goes a long way.

#62 – Two myths and two truths about change: 1. change will go away, when the truth is that change is here to stay. 2. You can just keep on doing what you have been doing, when the truth is that if your world is changing, you will have to change as well.

#63 – Three lessons: 1. To get what you've never had, you must do what you've never done – **be open**; 2. Tenacity is easier when you have no choice – **persist**; 3. Life is not measured by the number of breaths we take, but by the moments that take our breath away – **say yes.**

– The young consultant should strive to accomplish these six tasks: 1. Know yourself – know who you are and what is important to you; 2. Become an expert – develop knowledge and skills people need and will pay you to do; 3. Establish your style – work in a manner that is both comfortable and productive; 4. Build a network – be generous and helpful in service to others; 5. Create a cushion – for every dollar earned, invest a percentage for economic security; 6. Be true to your values – integrity is the indispensable element of consulting success.

#64 – In times of stress, stay focused, think clearly, act decisively.

#65 – 1. Keep backup files for courses and clients. 2. lock all home, car, and office doors. 3. Avoid crashes but be like the phoenix as all consultants must rise again.

Appendix D

Timeline and Code (biography, principles, relationships, cases)

B – Biography
- B #1 The early years – Philosophy and Psychology as foundational disciplines
- B #2 The second most important year of my life, 1963-64 – University of Vienna, Oscar Robertson, Viktor Frankl, and Israeli Kibbutzim
- B #3 False start in Arkansas and UC (University of Cincinnati) salvation
- B #4 Lucien Cohen, I/O (Industrial/Organizational) Psychology, and Eureka on I-75!
- B #5 First challenge to teach – from swimming pool lifeguard to University of Cincinnati/University of Dayton instructor (with Jenny Bean out of sight)
- B #6 Stress interview – General Motors and Ralph Nader (failure and lessons learned)
- B #7 Graduation and first adult job – Cincinnati Milacron, Kroger, and Ford (I go with Ford under false pretenses)
- B #8 The most important year of my life, 1967 – profession-

al work, marriage with children, new baby, first home, UC (University of Cincinnati) doctoral program
- B #9 Mistakes of commission – the Ford years
- B #10 The third most important year of my life, 1970 – Executive General, NKU (Northern Kentucky University), and life as I have known it for 52 years
- B #16 The brain, the terrain, and creating your future – Ben Carson's story
- B #33 The 4th most important year of my life, 2000 – the stern and craggy shores of Maine
- B #56 A nod to Freud
- B #61 Don't take yourself too seriously
- B #60 Golf course pearls – make your last work your best work

P – Principles
- P #11 Five early decisions that proved to be good
- P #12 The absolute need to live and work by five core principles for consulting success
- P #13 The importance of questions
- P #14 How teaching helps consulting and vice-versa
- P #18 The asexual consultant
- P #21 Number one consulting skill – time management
- P #28 The consultant image – the eye of the beholder
- P #29 Reality and humble pie
- P #31 Evaluation criteria for consulting services – pace, relevance, value, participation
- P #32 Joe Ward, Jimmy Stewart, and the Toyota news story – the power of the pen
- P #34 Using outdoor initiatives as a personal growth/OD (Organizational Development) tool – limits, liabilities, and testimonials
- P #35 Consulting for trade – barbecue ribs, hotel hospital-

ity, and dental care
- P #36 Attention and effort – work to learn/work to remember
- P #37 SERDI (Southeast Regional Directors Institute) lifelong learning – 911, Government Accounting 101, and Virginia's Black Box
- P #38 Dodging Stones – Courts, Corrections, and CitiCorp
- P #40 Be a learner – the importance of books
- P #41 Every consultant's dilemma – how much to charge
- P #42 Records count – keep them!
- P #43 Consultant-client compact
- P #44 The fit consultant
- P #45 The need for mindfulness
- P #49 Bridging the gap between theory and practice
- P #50 Managing human capital
- P #51 Technology challenges
- P #52 The theory and practice of leadership – balance is best
- P #53 Problem solving and human relations – two magic keys (the skeleton key/the master key)
- P #54 Murphy's Law
- P #58 How writing helps consulting and vice-versa
- P #62 Coping with change – the path of life and a book
- P #63 Career advice – straight shots, zig zags, and loop arounds
- P #64 Handling stressful situations
- P #65 Unexpected loss and the Phoenix Phenomenon – from overhead projector to flash drive

R – Relationships

- R #15 Working unfettered – consulting success and the ghost in the machine

- R #17 Consulting partnerships where one and one is more than two
- R #30 Be a continuous learner (every teacher needs a teacher)
- R #46 Client personalities
- R #47 No turtle ever got on a fencepost by itself – staff support
- R #48 Diversity as a strength
- R #57 My best two leaders

C – Cases
- C #19 My list of mosts
- C #20 Large scale consulting
- C #22 The Stabilus story – cross cultural communication and business success, including the SPOT (**S**uperior **P**roducts **o**n **T**ime) manifesto
- C #23 Train the trainer initiatives
- C #24 Going Hollywood – Sara Lee, Dolly Parton, and the stress of change (summer in the dark room)
- C #25 Most stressful groups
- C #26 What I didn't know that I wish I did know
- C #27 Be prepared – the motto of a good scout (the importance of knowing a day in the life of the client)
- C #39 Stretched in Nashville – the night it couldn't be done
- C #55 Maine projects and activities
- C #59 The Red River Leadership Institute – the strength of a region (building community without losing culture)

Index

A.
Acadia National Park 125
AI 175
American Society of Training and
    Development 95
Animals, pets 23
Appalachian Trail - 207
Armed forces, U. S. 13, 58, 59, 64, 117
Attorneys 101
Authors, leaders, and public figures –
    Adler, Alfred 48
    Aesop 123
    Allport, Gordon 44, 48, 214
    Alter, David 207
    Argyris, Chris 45, 211
    Aristotle 1, 211
    Barker, Joel 79, 117, 212
    Bellman, Geoffrey 3, 217
    Bennis, Warren 45, 210, 212
    Blanchard, Ken 45, 142, 214
    Bryson, Bill 207
    Burns, Robert 183
    Capote, Truman 74
    Carson, Ben 51, 52, 53, 54, 243
    Chanakya 1
    Churchill, Winston 36
    Collins, Jim 45, 79, 117, 209, 210
    Crosby, Phillip 96
    Darwin, Charles 200
    Deming, W. Edwards 45, 96
    Dewey, John 116, 210

Disney, Walt 111, 123
Drucker, Peter 2, 45, 79, 117, 213, 214
Eastwood, Clint 198
Edison, Thomas 112
Einstein, Albert 117
Erikson, Erik 48, 213
Florida, Richard 102
Frankl, Viktor 6, 7, 8, 15, 48, 53, 115,
    141, 142, 156, 211, 242
Franklin, Benjamin 36, 50, 88, 209
Freud, Sigmund 47, 187, 211
Fromm, Erich 48, 100, 213
Gandhi, Kasturba 114
Gandhi, Mohandas 114, 135
Gardner, John 122, 212
Gellerman, Saul 45, 212
Greenleaf, Robert 45, 186, 212
Greiner, Larry 3, 217
Heilbroner, Robert 29, 43, 170, 214
Heraclitus 201
Hertzberg, Frederick 45
Holmes Jr., Oliver Wendell 15, 203
Holtz, Lou 66
Horney, Karen 48, 212
James, William 169, 214
Joan of Arc 36
Jobs, Steve 53
Jung, Carl 48, 211
Juran, Joseph 96
Keith, Toby 198
Kennedy, John 8

Levinson, Harry 45, 210
Lewin, Kurt 45, 169
Likert, Rensis 45, 212
Lincoln, Abraham 1, 15, 112, 129, 179, 188, 211
Lippitt, Gordon 45
Lovecraft, H. P. 164
Marinoff, Lou 40, 212
Marx, Karl 15
Maslow, Abraham 45, 48, 212, 214
Massey, Morris 53, 214
Mayo, Elton 45
McClary, Clebe 66
McGregor, Douglas 2, 45, 213
McKinsey, James 2
McRaven, William 54, 211
Menninger, William 45
Mercury, Freddie 66
Merlin 1
Milton, John 119
Mintzberg, Henry 45, 214
Morris, Tom 119, 211
Moses 36
Moses, Grandma 13
Nader, Ralph 19
Niebuhr, Reinhold 104
Nietzsche, Friedrich 125
Odiorne, George 45, 211
Parton, Dolly 98
Perls, Fritz 48
Rigsby, Rick 54
Robertson, Oscar 6, 9, 130
Roger Rabbit 113
Rogers, Carl 47, 48, 212
Rogers, Will 41, 158
Roosevelt, Eleanor 36, 207
Roosevelt, Theodore 27
Rosenthal, Elizabeth 100
Rowling, J. K. 53
Russell, Bertrand 5, 141
Samuelson, Paul 29, 43, 170, 210

Schein, Edgar 45, 212
Schultz, Duane 47, 210, 214
Schwarzkopf Jr, Norman 66
Selye, Hans 117, 193, 212, 214
Skinner, B. F. 70, 215
St. Francis, of Assisi 138
Tassi, Nina 88
Taylor, Frederick 45, 214
Teresa, Mother 112
Thoreau, Henry David 118
Tolstoy, Leo 135
Truman, Harry 179
Twain, Mark 40, 145, 178, 188, 213
Ulmer, Walter 116, 208
Victoria, Queen 36
Walton, Sam 82
Welles, Orson 113
White, Robert 3, 211
Wooden, John 208, 215
Yeats, William Butler 115
Young, Fred 53, 145
Zimmerman, Alan 119
Angel Calvary 104

B.

Baptist Church 187
Behaviorism 5, 48
Behavior Modification 31, 123, 150
Books 209 –
A History of Western Philosophy 5
A Walk in the Woods 207
An American Sickness 100
Art of Leadership, The 36, 60, 93, 138, 191, 193, 197, 200
Behave 209
Body Keeps the Score, The 213
Building Community 58, 95, 122, 190, 192
Contemporary Consultant, The 3, 217
Consultant's Calling, The 3, 217, 222, 223, 224, 226
Economics 29, 143, 170, 210

Human Side of Work (series) 35, 81, 82, 93, 94, 191, 192
In Cold Blood 74
Lives in Progress 3, 211
Man's Search for Meaning 7, 53, 141, 142, 211
One Minute Manager, The 142, 214
Stress: Living and Working in a Changing World 117, 191, 192
Stress Without Distress: Rx for Burnout 153, 212
Worldly Philosophers, The 29, 43, 170, 214
Boy Scouts 187

C.
Career advice 202
CFOs 103
Change 61, 85, 92, 93, 98, 114, 184, 186, 193, 194, 200, 201
Cincinnati Enquirer 63
City Managers 102
Clients –private sector
AFL-CIO 34, 71
American Electric Power 81,82, 185
AT&T 35, 36, 61, 92, 132
ATE Management Systems 34
Audio Visual Network 98
Bangor Savings Bank 185
Bank of Oklahoma 183
Baptist, Catholic, Jewish, Methodist, and University HealthCare Systems 35
Beverly Enterprises 75
Bluegrass Foods 108
Cardinal Hill Hospital 83
Casco Bay CVB 185
Choice Hotels 63, 131
Cianbro Companies, The 62, 129, 182, 184, 185, 186
Cincinnati Children's Hospital 109
Cincinnati Milacron 21, 120
Citicorp 137

Commonwealth Hotels 63, 185
Correction Corporation of America (CoreCivic) 77, 82
Duke Energy 35, 36
Embry-Riddle Aeronautical University 79
EMERA 185
Frisch's 63
General Electric 24,
Great American Insurance 35, 65, 66
Health Alliance 77, 84, 85, 185
Hilliard Lyons 74
IBM 35, 61, 62, 74, 92, 96, 97, 112, 119, 145, 154, 155, 157
Independent Anesthesiologists 109
Jackson Lab 185
Johnson & Johnson 35, 117
Kahn's Sara Lee 98
King Kwik Markets 29, 31, 32, 136
Kroger Company 21, 29, 35, 36, 62, 92, 94
LifeNet-Air Methods 79
Maine Public Broadcasting Network 185, 186
Marion Merrell Dow 74, 80
Marriott 35, 36, 74, 92, 96
Martin's Point 185
Montgomery Inn 130, 131
Northern Light Health 186
Radisson Hotels 131
Sun Oil Company 29, 31
Tastemaker 64
Ten Broeck 127
Texoma Medical Center 182
Tri Health 77, 84, 85
UAW 26, 34, 69, 70, 71, 141
University of Cincinnati Medical College 109
Urology Group 137
Van Melle 128
VHA New England 185
West Shell Real Estate 69

Witham Family Hotels 185,186
Clients – Professions and Associations
Airports Council International 34, 74, 79
American Association of Airline Executives 79
American Medical Association 35, 100
American Public Transportation Association 34, 95
Association for Quality and Participation 35, 98
Illinois City/County Management Association 102
International Association of Convention and Visitor Bureaus 74, 185
International City/County Management Association 102
Kentucky Bar Association 101
Maine Development Foundation 184, 185
National Association of County Officials 102
National Association of Real Estate License Law Officials 69
Red River Leadership Institute 196, 197
SERDI (SouthEast Regional Directors Institute) 135
University of North Carolina – Public Executive Leadership Academy 102
Young Presidents Organization 46
Clients – Public Sector
Airports – Cincinnati, Cleveland, Denver, Dulles, Indianapolis, Lehigh Valley, Washington, D.C. 34, 79
Barren River Area Development District 110
Bluegrass Area Development District 128
City of Covington 64
Clermont County 77, 85, 86, 137
Commonwealth of Kentucky 35, 77
Connecticut Department of Transportation 56
Criminal Justice – Ohio, Kentucky, Indiana, Florida 34, 93
Delaware Department of Transportation 156
Eastern Kentucky University 93
Federal Aviation Administration 34, 77
Florida Department of Corrections 182
Indiana Department of Corrections 58, 59, 67, 182
Internal Revenue Service 93
Kentucky Department of Corrections 59
Kentucky Governor's Cabinet 78
Kentucky Human Resources Cabinet 72
Kentucky Human Rights Commission 57
Kentucky Legislative Research Commission 78
Kentucky State University 107
Maine Department of Education 185
Maine School Management Association 186
Maine State Police 185, 186
National Institutes of Health (NIH) 64, 69, 70, 117
North Carolina State University 62, 126
Queen City Metro 92, 95
Tennessee Human Rights Commission 57
Transportation Authority of Northern Kentucky (TANK) 123
U. S. Military 13, 58, 59, 64, 117
United States Navy 13, 35
University of North Carolina – Chapel Hill 102
Coaching 30, 35, 150, 173, 175, 176
Colleagues –
Ablassmeir, Michael 194
Aerni, Al 120
Anderson, Jim 110
Attenweiler, Bill 3, 18
Austin, Al 72, 73

Bailey, Steve 163, 185
Baker, Alan 208
Barnhart, Gordon 126, 223
Barone, Nancy 204
Barron, Gordon 6
Barton, Dennis 94
Bean, Jenny 17
Bennett, Don 95
Bennett, Mike 129
Berry, Susan 185
Bhatta, Krishna 208
Biernat, John 193
Black, Tom 162
Blair, Mendy 163
Bonar-Stewart, Terri 64, 95, 117, 161
Boyle, Dick 81, 82, 161, 223
Bridenbaugh, Phil 109
Brooks, Mark 64, 129, 162, 208
Brooks, Steve 86
Brothers, Doug 86
Brownfield, Irene 165
Buncher, Mike 110
Burton, Alan 62, 161
Burton, Barry 103
Buss, Ed 182
Cahall, Jack 120
Campbell, Mike 56, 227
Caplon, Bob 53, 61, 163
Carlisle, Wayne 162, 227
Chesnut, Jeff 118
Clark, David 86
Collins, Martha Layne 72, 73, 77, 78, 185
Cook, Jack 185, 227
Creevy, Joe 137
Cummings, Jim 123
Curtis, Kent 55, 60, 63, 191
Datta, Yudister 167
Davis, Vaughn 95
DeMille, Stan 191
Desai, Tripta 167
Dohan, Alan 29, 227

Donahue, David 58, 63
Dorsey, Martha 86
Dorsey, Roy 165
Dow, Jim 185
Downing, Evan 118
Drubel, Charles v
Ducker, Gavin 185
Duke, Gordon 72, 220
Elicker, Ed 137
Eversole, Jack 110
Fay, Dan 185
Followell, Rob 64, 144, 162
Futrell, Jennifer 118, 165, 193
Gausvik, Chris 183
Gebbie, Bill 9
Gibbons, Dan 98
Gibson, Paul 94
Gilliam, Fred 162
Gillihan, Kerry 62, 83, 162
Gregorie, Dan 65, 124, 163, 185
Grimshaw, Roger 28
Guarino, Kellie 184
Gunkel, Ken iii
Hacke, Harry 141
Haghkerdar, Kaveh 208
Hanf, Bob 185
Harvey, Ed 95
Harwood, Bill 163, 185
Hewett, Chuck 162
Hinckley, Pat 182
Holbrook, Tim 162
Holloway, Bill 28, 87
Holmes, Chuck 63
Hosea, David 162
Houchin, Steve 94
Howes, David 185
Hun, Nicholas iv
Hunter, Gerald 62, 163
Jablonski, Paul 95
Jackson, Richard 162
Jones, Florence 162
Jordan, Pete 63, 219

Keefe, Dan 185, 223
Kinney, Miranda 118
Kirk, Patrick 63, 157
Kouneski, Tony 95
Krings, David 102, 225
Kumar, Vinay 167
Larson, Larry iv
Lawrence, Ray 123
Leffler, Charles 62, 126, 162
LeMaster, Bill 71
Lewis, Phil 94
Linder, Al 63
Lindsay, Bill 116
Link, Fred 163, 185
Linnes, Erhard 6
Longo, Bobbi 9
Lovenberg, Walter 64, 69, 70, 80, 162
Luria, Joe 109
Lyman, Ginger 83
Lyons, Kathy 165
Mann, Sarah 118
Marriott, J. W. 96
Martin, Steve 116, 220
McClary, Clebe 66
McCollister, John 87
McGrath, Joe 185
McLaughlin, Jim 94
McMillen, Steve 59, 63, 117, 126, 224
Miller, Cyndy 163
Miller, Mary Helen 78
Monnig, Bill 137
Nassar, Nassar 138
Noel, Tony 138
Ohren, Joe 60, 105
Park, Dick 109
Payne, Mitchell iv
Petrick, Joe 117
Pfaff, Pam 165
Piazza, Larry 157
Price, Joe 191
Quealy, Paul 64, 120, 223
Quirk, Bob 29

Ramundo, Mike 120
Raskin, Roy 96
Rawlings, Melody iv
Rees, John 59, 63, 163, 221
Richards, Jerry 117
Richeson, Dave 90, 163
Ronay, Dan 58, 59, 162, 182
Rubendall Susan 193
Ruddy, Richard 110
Rudel, Mary Beth 197
Russell, George 78
Saric, Alan 162
Schulte, Vince 189
Scott, Bret 63
Seal, Ron 62, 161, 182
Sederberg, George 120
Sekhon, Jas 128, 163, 167
Setzer, Mike 95
Shah, Jiten 167
Shank, Matthew 227
Shottelkotte, Al 123
Sippola, Carlene 193
Sizemore, Gil 141
Snyder, Gordy 63, 162, 185
Spell, Laura 194
Sprouse, Dave 61
Steely, Frank 29
Stenberg, Carl 102, 163
Stone, Bob 93
Stone, Cliff 148, 165
Strong, Robert 208
Swanson, Terri 163, 185
Taylor, Bob 156
Taylor, Jim 185
Tesseneer, Ralph 189
Theriault, Jim 163, 185
Thomes, Barb 118, 165
Tierney, Brian 81, 185
Tillotson, Lynn 185
Tripp, David 185
Turner, Jimmy 63, 82
Ulmer, Walter 116, 208

Utly, Harold 191
Vaidya, Ashish 167
Van Melle, Marius 128, 227
Vanderburg, Bill 185
Vigue, Andi 129
Vigue, Peter 129, 161, 208
Vinci, Sam 31, 136
Von Zychlin, Claus 185, 227
Votruba, Jim 180
Wagner, John 94, 221
Walker, Lindsey 118, 165, 194
Walter, Jeff 65, 162, 227
Walz, Earl 137, 141
Ward, Joe 122
Warren, Kevin 118, 193
Washburn, Paula vi
Washington, Michael 95, 225
Wasson, Cathy 165
Watts, Beverly 57, 95, 225
Wehrspann, Susan 61, 118, 163
Whalen, Greg 111
Wharton, Steve 86
Wilhelm, Stella 69
Williams, John 123
Williams, Linda 165
Winston, Andy 193
Wolfe, Rick 69
Wones, Robert 157
Woodward, Angie 163, 184
Woychik, Rick 185
Wyler, Stephanie 86
Xiao, Ling iii
Youngquist, Jim 63, 161, 196
Zimmerman, Omi 8
Communications 37, 62, 122
Consulting –
  Cancellation 144
  Compact 149, 150, 151
  Coordination 132, 151
  Cost 143, 144, 145, 146
  Definition 1

Evaluation 120, 121
Health 153, 154, 155, 156, 157
  for trade 130, 131, 132
Human relations 17, 37, 68, 178, 179
Humility 66, 129, 132, 199
Image 111, 112, 113
Industry 1, 2
Large scale 77
Lessons learned 229
Mindfulness 159
Mistakes 25, 26, 27
Morality 40, 69, 96, 117
Partnerships 55, 61
Planning 170
Preparation 27, 133, 143, 181
Principles 39
Problem solving 178
Records 37, 148
Regimen 37
Skill 87
Success 39
Types 1
Virtual 118, 144

D.

Dissertation – *Predictors of Success for*
    Million Dollar Round Table Members
    33
Delta Airlines 78
Diversity 37, 58, 95, 167

E.

Ethics 35, 36, 67, 69, 96, 116, 117, 170,
  194 –
  Business 96
  Executive General 28, 29

F.

Family –
  Bill, grandson 125
  Earl, father 187

Heather, daughter 22, 125, 207
Jessie, granddaughter 75, 125
Larry, son 22, 24, 124, 125
Nancy, wife 21, 22, 23, 24, 26, 49, 50, 74, 76, 124, 125, 131, 139, 157, 193
Page, son 22, 24, 125
Ruth, mother 187
Ford Motor Company 21, 22, 25, 26, 28, 70, 141 –
 Associates 25
 Ford, Henry 27
 Labor Relations 25, 26, 28
 Sharonville 28, 71

G.
Gallup 172, 173
General Motors 19, 20, 105
Google, project oxygen 176 –
 Oxygen 176
Gun and knife show 105, 107

H.
Hidden agenda 106
Hollywood 98, 130
Human Capital 172, 173
Human Relations 17, 19, 40, 68, 114, 125, 179
Human resource management 95
Humanistic Psychology 5, 47, 48
Humility 66, 129, 132, 199

I.
Institute of European Studies 6

J.

K.
Kellogg 12
Kibbutzim 6, 10

L.
Labor Relations 25, 26, 27, 28, 33
Leadership 19, 21, 36, 37, 57, 59, 60, 62, 63, 64, 65, 66, 81, 82, 83, 85, 116, 122, 156, 172, 185, 186, 194
Leadership Today 194
Locations –
 Athens 7
 Arkansas 12, 196
 Bermuda 74, 154
 Black Forest 154
 Boulder 157
 Cape Elizabeth 184
 Chicago 7, 103
 Delaware 156
 Detroit 19, 26, 51, 102
 Europe 6, 208
 Greece 10
 Hafalakar 9
 Hamilton 17
 Hawaii 74, 112, 154
 Israel 6, 10
 Istanbul 10
 Jerusalem 7
 Kaprun 9
 Middletown 9, 187
 Nashville 138
 New York 6, 112
 Ozark 13
 Piqua 17
 Prague 9, 10
 Puerto Rico 154, 192
 Rockland 184
 Rome 7, 10
 San Diego 102
 St. John 154, 192
 Strasbourg 80
 Troy 17
 Tucson 71
 Turkey 10
 Vicksburg 154
 Virginia 35, 68, 135, 154

Vienna 6, 7, 8, 9, 10, 11
Williamsburg 135, 154
Washington, D.C. 61, 69, 79, 113, 154
Leadership development –
  Experienced and emerging leadership development 58
  Leadership Kentucky 184
  Kentucky Power – American Electric Power 81
  Red River Leadership Institute 196, 197
  Cianbro Companies, The 62, 129, 182, 184, 185, 186
  Union 34, 71
Louisville Courier-Journal 122

M.

Maine 124, 125, 154, 184
Management education 27, 35, 64, 96
Megatrends 98
McGraw-Hill 138, 175, 193, 194 –
  Ablassmeir, Mike 194
  Biernat, John 193
  Clare, Debbie 194
  Granger, Lisa 194
  Hurd, Amelia 194
  Kusper, Hannah 194
  MacNaughton, Hannah 194
  Spell, Laura 194
  Vogt, Karryn 194
  Walker, Lindsey 118, 165, 194
  Winston, Andy 193
Mindfulness 159
Mistakes 25, 26, 27
Money management 46, 144, 145, 146
Morale 3, 14, 15, 30, 35, 71, 81, 95, 104, 110, 117, 122, 150, 170
Mormon Tabernacle 66
Motivation 2, 35, 126, 209
Murphy's Law 181 –
  Florida Department of Corrections 182
  Indiana Department of Corrections 182
  Texoma Medical Center 182

Cianbro Companies, The 62, 129, 182, 184, 185, 186

N.

Northern Kentucky University (NKU) 28, 44, 51, 66, 103, 111, 131

O.

Organizational development 126, 150
Organizational Psychology (also industrial/organizational psychology) 14, 19, 45
Syllabus, Organizational Consulting 216
Outdoor initiatives 126, 127—
Outward Bound 126

P.

Participative management 96, 97, 117, 151
Peace Corps 12
Phoenix phenomenon 205
Physicians 100
Preparation 74, 92, 109, 110, 133, 181–
  Barren River Area Development District 110
  Bluegrass Foods 108
  Cincinnati Children's Hospital 109
  Independent Anesthesiologists 109
Philosophy 5, 7, 15, 19, 39, 115, 117, 119, 198
Positive Psychology 47
Productivity 88
Psychology 5, 12, 13
Psychoanalysis 5, 48

Q.

Quality 35, 56, 96
Questions, importance 41

R.

Red Bus trip 105

S.

Savant Learning Systems 138, 139, 193
Seminars and Talks –
  Building Community 58, 84, 95, 122, 192, 196
  Building Your Personal Infrastructure 102
  Caring Leadership 36, 156
  Leading Change 98, 193
  Leading Quality 56
  Managing the Stress of Being a lawyer 36, 101
  Our Summit Awaits 132
  Professional Wellbeing 100
South-Western Publishing 191, 192
Stress 19, 35, 37, 76, 88, 92, 98, 100, 101, 103, 117, 153, 155, 192, 193, 204, 205–
  CFO stress 103
  Groups 100, 101, 102
  Interview 19
  Physician stress 100
  Selye, Hans 117, 193, 212, 214
Skilled trades 27
Spring Grove Cemetery 22, 24
SPOT 91
Stabilus 90, 91
Syllabus, Organizational Consulting 216

T.

Teachers (mentors)115 –
  Brooks, Jim 25
  Cohen, Lucien 14, 15, 19, 21, 115
  Frankl, Viktor 6, 7, 8, 15, 48, 53, 115, 141, 142, 156, 211, 242
  Mowatt, Edward 6, 7, 115
  Steinhaus, Arthur 115
  Stewart, Bill 17, 18, 19, 21, 115
Teaching 29, 34, 43, 45, 115 –
  Behavior Theory and Business Practice 45
  Economics 29

Humanistic Psychology 47, 48
Management and Organization 44
Small Business Management 46
T-Group Theory and Laboratory Method 47
Teams 116
Teamsters 69, 71
Technology 117, 174, 196
Tibetan Secret 158
Time management 37, 87, 88, 93
Toyota 73, 122
Train the trainer initiatives 35, 92, 93, 94

U.

University of Cincinnati 13, 14, 17, 19, 22, 109, 157
Upjohn 12

V.

Values, Study of –
  Allport, Vernon, and Lindsey 44
Vienna 6, 7, 8, 9, 10, 11 –
  Boys' choir 11
  University 8, 9, 11
  Opera 11
  Symphony 11
Vision 79, 117
Viet Nam 13

W.

Walmart 82
Whole Person Press 193

Y.

YMCA 187
Young Presidents Organization (YPO) 46

About the Author

George Manning is professor emeritus of psychology at Northern Kentucky University. He is a consultant to business, industry, and government, serving such clients as the AMA, AT&T, General Electric, IBM, Duke Energy, the United Auto Workers, Young Presidents' Organization, the U.S. Navy, and the National Institutes of Health. He lectures on economic and social issues, including quality of work-life, workforce values, and business ethics. He maintains an active program of research and writing in organizational psychology. His current studies and interests include the changing meaning of work, leadership ethics, and coping skills for personal and social change.